Prophet Muḥammad
THE TEACHER

صلى الله عليه وسلم

Prophet Muḥammad
THE TEACHER

by ʿAbd al-Fattāḥ Abū Ghuddah

Translated by the late author's son:
Ustādh Muḥammad Zāhid Abū Ghuddah

AWAKENING

PUBLISHED BY THE PRESS SYNDICATE OF AWAKENING PUBLICATIONS
Uplands Business Centre, Bernard Street, Swansea, SA2 0DR
United Kingdom

AWAKENING PUBLICATIONS
Uplands Business Centre, Bernard Street, Swansea, SA2 0DR
United Kingdom
P.O. Box 360009, Milpitas, CA 95036, United States of America

First Published in January 2017

Typeset in Sabondiactritic
Printed by Mega Printing in Turkey

Prophet Muhammad: The Teacher
by Shaykh 'Abd al-Fattāh Abū Ghuddah
Translated by Muhammad Zāhid Abū Ghuddah
Edited by Yasrab Dawud Shah

p. cm.
Includes bibliographical references
ISBN: 978-1-905837-18-2
1. Islam - - Theories. 1. Title.
BP65.G7M37 2002
297.049109031- 97-41874 CIP

بسم الله الرحمن الرحيم

SHAYKH ʿABD AL-FATTĀḤ ABŪ GHUDDAH was born in Syria in 1917. One of the outstanding Muslim scholars of the 20th century, Shaykh Abū Ghuddah was a leading scholar in the field of ḥadīth and Ḥanafī school of fiqh. He studied in Syria and Egypt specialising in Arabic language, ḥadīth, sharīʿah, and psychology. He had many prominent teachers, among them Shaykh Rāghib al-Tabbākh, Shaykh Aḥmad ibn Muḥammad al-Zarqa, Shaykh ʿĪsā al-Bayanūnī, Shaykh Aḥmad al-Kurdī, and the renowned Ottoman Scholar Imām al-Kawtharī. He taught *uṣūl al-fiqh*, Ḥanafī *fiqh* and Comparative *fiqh* at the University of Damascus. He also taught at the King Saud University and Imām Muḥammad ibn Saud Islamic University. He was buried in al-Baqīʿ cemetery in Madinah 1997.

CONTENT

FOREWORD

Praise is only for Allah who is the Lord of the entire creation and the Master of the universe and peace and blessings be upon Muḥammad al-Muṣtafa who was sent as a mercy for all humankind, upon his family and his followers.

The need of the day is for us to follow the best of all teachers who taught us how to live a righteous and pious life and seek the pleasure of Allah. We are in dire need to get to know and understand him as the fountain of knowledge, science, wisdom, morality, love, compassion, benevolence and mercy.

When the young Hasan al-Banna - whom I've know from the time he was still at school - informed me that he was publishing the translated work of Abdul Fattāḥ Abū Ghuddah (may Allah's mercy be upon him) on the Prophetic methods of teaching, my heart grew in pride not just because I have had the privilege of observing Hasan's pious father guide him and provide a loving Islamic home environment to nurture his considerable talents but also because I admire the way he has made such wise choices in taking full advantage of the many educational opportunities available to all those who Allah has sent to live in this part of the global village. The fact is that there are so many rich and varied treasures in the Arabic language which I, along with a disproportionately large part of the

Ummah of Muḥammad ﷺ, am deprived of and any effort to raise our awareness has to be greatly appreciated.

I have of course read other translations of this important work but Ustadh Zahid Abu Ghuddah's translation of his esteemed father's work has managed to convey a more thorough and detailed insight. It has enhanced the clarity of this all-important subject with his uniquely personal flow to thrill the reader into motivation. It has spurred me even further towards ensuring that the world of education delves more meticulously into the Prophetic teaching methodologies which cross all borders of time and space and thereby benefit from this eternal fountain of knowledge. I am astonished how little of this perfection is known by the educationalists I have worked with over the years. We Muslims are fond of blaming the secularists, the western media, the orientalists and anyone else we can define as the 'enemy' of Islam for this ignorance of the ways of our beloved Prophet. However we are reluctant to recognise the unacceptable levels of inadequacies and deficiencies within our own ranks. In an unapologetically secular world we cannot blame those who are influenced by ideas that are well articulated, effectively disseminated and role models which are attractively presented as celebrities and examples of success.

We as Muslim educationists have so far been demonstrably ineffective in finding ways to present the Prophet ﷺ as the best, noble and all encompassing humanitarian role model to the world. Too often the Muslim world turns towards the West in seeking the best way to educate future generations and often ignores the fact that "the best" in fact lies in the Jewel of Islam – within the framework of the Qur'an and the Sunnah of the Prophet ﷺ. I am sure that this book will inspire Muslim teachers to aim towards emulating the ways of the Prophet Muḥammad in becoming role models for their learners and using the Prophetic teachings in helping them to learn more effectively. It should help educators to be teachers who hold their caring hands over the heads of learners, opening their minds with creative imagination and touching their hearts with compassion.

This translation will no doubt be a source of benefit for all who are desirous of raising standards and aiming for educational excellence. Those who, like me, have received their higher education in England or who are familiar with contemporary English language terminology in the field of education will be able to identify the basic concepts embedded in the text with ease. For example when the author describes the "individual differences among students" the idea of differentiation, individualised and personalised learning will readily come to mind. Similarly while you read through the book, page after page, chapter after chapter you will realise that it is infused with 'a broad and balanced curriculum', 'essential core skills for life', 'outcome based learning', 'problem based child centred learning', 'strategic planning with clear learning outcomes and targets', 'creative and effective teaching', 'assessment informed teaching techniques and lesson planning', 'cognitive and metacognitive processes', 'school and community engagement', 'collaborative learning', 'critical thinking skills', 'activity based learning', 'computer or ICT supported learning', 'learning by teaching', 'informal, enquiry-based or co-operative learning', 'opening minds approach to education', 'teacher as a role model', 'spiritual, moral and emotional aspects of personal development', 'life long learning', 'discipline', 'social cohesion', 'integration', 'social justice, 'equality', ... and many more buzz words of the educational landscape today.

There is no doubt that the solution to ignorance and misunderstanding lies at the core of an enlightened Islamic education. Perhaps the younger generation of educationalists amongst the readers of this book who have the command of both English &

Arabic languages will take up the challenge and fulfil the dreams of deficient educators like me by translating more of the rich treasures of our Islamic heritage. May Allah reward everyone involved in this project for their efforts and give us all the ability to follow the example of our beloved Prophet Muḥammad ﷺ.

Mohammed Akram Khan-Cheema OBE
Former Chief Inspector of Schools in Bradford, UK

INTRODUCTION

To introduce a book by the eminent scholar, Shaykh 'Abdul Fattah Abu Ghuddah, is humbling. Shaykh Abu Ghuddah was not only a master in all of the major Islamic disciplines; he was also a meticulous researcher and a prolific writer. Hence, his books and commentaries display a depth of erudition that is rarely found in contemporary Islamic scholarship. Furthermore, to introduce a book dealing with any aspect of the character, example, or the ontological reality of our Prophet Muhammad ﷺ, is even more humbling. It is truly a daunting challenge to prepare the readers for the benefit conveyed by such an eminent scholar, from our Prophet ﷺ.

Hence, when I was contacted by Hasan al-Banna, a credible scholar himself, to write an introduction to Shaykh Muhammad Zahid Abu Ghuddah's translation of a great Arabic work authored by his father, Shaykh Abdul Fattah Abu Ghuddah, *Ar-Rasul al-Mu'allim* (Prophet Muhammad: The Teacher), I was greatly honored, yet equally humbled. The honor lies in being chosen for a task that would connect my name, even in a small way with that of such a luminous scholar. Similarly, it is a great honor to be able to provide a service that will assist in letting the world know of an aspect of the greatness of our Prophet, Muhammad ﷺ, at a time when his name, honor and message are being sullied in many quarters by ignorant or irreverent advocates of vile and nefarious agendas.

The humbling aspect of the request lies in the fact that I know my inadequacies and fear that I will not do justice to either a scholar of Shaykh Abu Ghuddah's stature, nor to the honor of our Prophet ﷺ. However, after much prayer and contemplation, I thought that were I to engage the task relying on Allah and trusting in the expansiveness of His Grace and Providence; that perhaps I could write something suitable.

The noted orientalist, Frantz Rosenthal, states in his acclaimed work, *Knowledge Triumphant: The Concept of Knowledge in Medieval Islam,* "In Islam, the concept of knowledge enjoyed an importance unparalleled in other civilizations."[1] Although this statement would be viewed as positive to most Muslims, Rosenthal fails to identify the source of the Prophet Muhammad's ﷺ deep respect for knowledge. Hence, finding no precedent for the Prophet's attitude in pre-Islamic Arabian society and culture, he concludes that it must be due to an "outside influence."[2] Not able to convincingly identify what that outside influence might be, and operating on the assumption that the Prophet ﷺ, fabricated the Qur'an, the best that Rosenthal can do is to posit that the Prophet ﷺ was inspired to place knowledge at the center of the Islamic enterprise because of the influence of Christian Gnostics.

As Muslims we know better. That "outside influence" is the Qur'an itself. It is not without purpose that the word knowledge ('ilm) and its derivatives occur approximately 750 times in the Qur'an. Allah, through the Qur'anic message was inculcating in the Prophet ﷺ the centrality of knowledge. This is so because through

---

[1] *Frantz Rosenthal, Knowledge Triumphant: The Concept of Knowledge in Islam Medieval Islam (Boston, Leiden: Brill, 2007), 334.*

[2] *Ibid., 23.*

the message he was vouchsafing for humanity, a new type of civilization was being brought into being. This unique civilization, unlike its predecessors and successors, would not be based on race, tribe, geography, language or class. It would be based on the possession and affirmation of knowledge. Hence, it would be a truly universal civilization, for membership in its ranks would be open to anyone who possessed and affirmed the knowledge undergirding it.

The most fundamental fact in that knowledge base, one that is indispensible for the development of a sound Muslim personality, is the knowledge of God and His Oneness. When this fact is introduced in the Qur'an, it is immediately associated with knowledge. Allah proclaims, *Know that there is no god but Allah, and seek forgiveness for your sins.* (Qur'an 47:19) This brief Qur'anic statement not only affirms that one must know of God's reality, to be considered a Muslim, but one must also act in a way that is consistent with that knowledge.

The most immediately relevant actions in this regard are those that assist us towards the attainment of salvation. These actions would include seeking forgiveness for our sins. However, they do not stop there and include all of those actions that constitute sincere service to Allah, and to our fellow humans. Concerning service to Allah, we are reminded in the Qur'an, *I have only created the Jinn and the humans that they worship me.* (Qur'an 51:56) The word "worship" in this context could reasonably be translated as "serve." As for our service to our fellow humans, we read, *You are the best of communities brought forth for humanity...* (Qur'an 4:110) The great commentator, Ibn Kathir mentions, on the authority of several righteous forebears, that the meaning of "*...for humanity*" in the verse just quoted, is "the most beneficial of humanity to their fellow humans."[3]

[3] *Ibn Kathir, Tafsir al-Qur'an al-'Adhim 3:110*

These twin endeavors occupying the heart of every sincere believer, serving Allah and serving humanity, have been the motors pushing the Muslim intellectual project forward.

For example, the sciences of mathematics, geometry, trigonometry, and astronomy were initiated by efforts to accurately determine the prayer direction (qibla) from lands far removed from Mecca. The advances made by Muslims in these areas were rooted in their desire to serve God.

The desire to understand and preserve the Qur'anic message gave birth to advances in grammar, rhetoric, syntax, phonetics, and general linguistics that predated the appearance of similar levels of knowledge in these areas elsewhere in the world by many centuries. Likewise, the desire to serve humanity urged the incredible advances that Muslim made in the fields of medicine, horticulture, irrigation, urban planning, architecture, law, sociology and many other spheres of endeavor. Finally, the desire to save people from being ruined by their four great enemies: the ego, Satan, the whims of the soul, and the seductiveness of the world, led to unparalleled advances in spirituality and moral psychology.

As Rosenthal and others correctly opine, the immediate starting point for the great intellectual achievements that were witnessed in Islamic civilization is the Prophet Muhammad ﷺ. Although he was illiterate, his greatest contribution to Islamic civilization, and through that portal to world civilization, is the Qur'an. The Qur'an not only places knowledge at the center of the quest for the good life and salvation, as we have alluded to above, it also introduces us to the idea of the Prophet Muhammad ﷺ as a teacher. This, of course, is the major theme guiding the meticulous scholarship displayed Shaykh Abu Ghuddah in this book.

To be a good teacher one has to have good instructors. At every stage of his development, the Prophet ﷺ had the best. He was educated by nature in the best of settings, the Arabian Desert. Here he was able to develop the spiritual and imaginative parameters that in latter life would lead to his desire to know his Lord and to work for the moral rectification of his people. As Jean-Jacques Rousseau discusses in *Emile*,[4] his highly acclaimed treatise on education, the natural state of a child is best preserved, during the earliest stages of his development, by nature. The Prophet ﷺ spent the early years of his life in a pristine desert environment that allowed him, in Rousseau's words to "run, jump, and shout," or to develop unhindered by the limitations imposed by more involved and complex societies. The Prophet's desert education ﷺ also allowed him reflect on the wonders he observed all around him: the stark beauty of the earth-tones in the desert sands surrounding him; the variegated rock formations intermeshing with the vast, brilliant, blue sky; the seemingly boundless canopy of the night sky adorned with brilliant stars that must have appeared too numerous to even begin counting, combined to leave an indelible imprint on his heart, mind and soul.

Upon leaving the desert and coming to the bustling town of Mecca, the Prophet ﷺ began another phase of his education. Again, he would have the best of teachers. He learned through keeping the company of his esteemed grandfather, Abdul Muttalib, and his uncle, Abu Talib, during this stage. Although both men were poor, they were among the leaders of their people, the Quraysh, and they were able to impart unto the Prophet ﷺ many valuable lessons in the various realms of life. Those lessons would avail him when he later began his career as a teacher to all of mankind.

This phase is one of observation, and not one that involves

---

[4] See Jean-Jacques Rousseau, Emile (New York: Basic Books, 1979), Book Two for Rousseau's discussion on the positive effect of a "natural" education during the early years of a child's life.

dealing with abstract ideas and theories. During this phase, which overlaps with the latter half of the second phase identified by Rousseau, the child begins to learn moral lessons and higher truths through observation. Here, the role models that a child has are critical, for they are planting seeds of understanding in his or her consciousness. Those seeds would blossom into the qualities that would make Prophet ﷺ as he moved into adult life, the most respected and trustworthy (al-Amin) member of his society.

That early education would lead him, as he matured into adulthood, to reject the idolatry of his people and to begin searching for ways to reform their society. He would seek to rid them of the many customs and habits that they were involved in. Some of these practices involved needless deaths, such as their odious practice of burying alive their female daughters, while others involved the usurpation of God-given rights. During this stage, the Prophet ﷺ began to reflect on higher ideas and concepts. Those ideas were related to the nature of man and the universe; the requisites of sound moral behavior, the place of God in His creation, the nature of the relationship between God and man, and related matters.

However, prior to his call to the prophetic office, any insight he might have been gained into these issues was not firm knowledge. He is described during this phase as being "astray." Allah mentions in the Qur'an, "*...and He found you astray and He guided you.*" (Qur'an 93:11) His straying involves him lacking firm knowledge concerning the details of the creed and practice of the monotheistic faith he and a few other "Hanifs," or monotheists were endeavoring to practice. Allah describes his state more clearly elsewhere in the Qur'an, *Thus have we sent unto you a spirit by our command. You did not know [before prophecy] neither revelation nor faith. However, we have made it* [the Qur'an] *a light wherewith we guide whosoever will desire of our servants. And verily, you guide to a* *straight path.* (Qur'an 42:52)

Having guided His Prophet ﷺ, Allah commanded him to teach others. He says, *...as for the grace of your Lord, proclaim it!* (Qur'an 93:11) One of the ways he had been blessed ﷺ, was with knowledge and divine guidance. One of the implications of the above command is that he is to share his knowledge with others. In fact, he is threatened with perdition were he to conceal anything of the knowledge his Lord blessed him with. We read in the Qur'an, *Those who conceal the clear signs and guidance we have revealed after we have clearly expounded them to humanity in the scripture; on them shall be the curse of Allah and all of those entitled to curse.* (Qur'an 2:159) As Shaykh Abu Ghuddah makes abundantly clear in the pages that follow, the Prophet ﷺ implemented the command that he teach in ways that were more varied and creative than anyone before or after him.

After introducing the reader to the character and personality of the Prophet ﷺ, specifically those that are relevant in aiding his efficacy as a teacher, Shaykh Abu Ghuddah details the various methodologies employed by the Prophet ﷺ. Those methodologies are extremely diverse, for the Prophet ﷺ, was a teacher of humanity. Hence, his students were young and old, rich and poor, learned and illiterate, free and in bondage, male and female, influential and powerless. They also represented various racial, ethnic and tribal groups.

To effectively teach them all, it is logical that the Prophet ﷺ, would utilize various methodologies as Shaykh Abu Ghuddah vividly details with ample examples from the Qur'an and the Sunnah, oftentimes accompanied by his own extensive commentary. Like the Qur'an itself, the Prophet ﷺ used repetition to encourage understanding and retention. Similarly, in Qur'anic fashion, he often employed gradualism as he allowed time for those he was instructing to slowly grasp the particulars of more involved or complex issues. At times he employed what could be described as a Socratic dialectical method. Sometimes he would emphasize rote memorization, while other times he would emphasize understanding. He was known to pose rhetorical questions. Sometimes he would answer questions in brief to encourage the student to expand on the ideas he was presenting. Sometimes he would engage in detailed commentary around a particular issue. He would not hesitate to use illustrations, and other forms of imagery. Sometimes he would use humor as an effective pedagogical tool, while other times he would couch the information he was presenting in grave seriousness. Oftentimes he would prepare the student for the information he intended to present with an elaborate introduction, while at other times he would immediate begin his presentation with little or no introduction. Sometimes he would broadcast a message, addressing a wide cross-section of the community, while other times he would narrowcast his message, restricting it to women, merchants, or other groups.

The Prophet ﷺ was also known to teach in a wide variety of settings, both formal and informal. He would teach in the masjid, in the desert, while riding on a mule, camel or donkey. He would teach while visiting the house of one of his companions or while on an expedition preparing for battle. All of these various situations illustrate the truthfulness of a claim he himself made ﷺ "I have only been sent as a teacher."[5]

As I have stated, Shaykh Abu Ghuddah deals with all of these issues with a range of source texts and a depth of analysis seldom found in contemporary Islamic scholarship. However, he alludes to something more important. If the Prophet ﷺ was the greatest teach-

[5] *Sunan Ibn Majah: 229*

er humanity has known, it behooves us to endeavor to understand the essence of the message he was conveying, for that message was not only shaping the hearts and minds of those he was teaching, it was also shaping him in ways that enhanced his desire and ability to teach.

He was not just teaching, he was reshaping human beings. This is not surprising for he described his mission in the following manner, "I was only sent to perfect good character."[6] The possessors of those reshaped characters would reform the world. Shaping hearts and minds, in a way that allows them to reengage the world from a totally different vantage point, is an integral part of an educational process referred to by Jack Mezirow as "transformative education."[7] This idea, in its broad overview, describes "...a praxis, a dialectic in which understanding and action interact to produce an altered state of being."[8]

In the Islamic worldview, the dialectic at the heart of the transformation brought about by education is comprised of knowledge (understanding) and worship (action). This combination in turn produces an altered state of being where the state of disbelief (kufr) is replaced by the state of belief (iman). As is the case with the argument made by advocates of transformative education, this altered state, when deep and widespread enough, can become the basis for transformations in the world.

There are many other parallels one could draw between theories of transformative education and Islam. For example, a person's commitment to a transformative learning group requires solidarity,

---

[6] *Bayhaqi, 20,782.*

[7] *Mezirow, J. (1991). Transformative dimensions in adult learning.San Francisco: Jossey-Bass.*

[8] *Ibid., xii.*

empathy, and trust.[9] These are all key elements in the formation of a coherent Ummah, or a wider community of Muslims. However, one should not stretch the similarities between this particular theory of education and Islam too far. For just as there are similarities between the two there are also differences.

One difference is that transformative education is not predicated on the existence of ultimate truths that one wishes to discover at the end of the process. Rather, the goal is to be open to further transformation in different contexts. This openness to further transformation is true to a point in Islam. As Muslims we accept that all of the contexts we might find ourselves undergoing a transformation in, such as family, community, place of employment, etc., are themselves governed by Islamic principles and rulings and hence there is a point, in this context, where our transformation stops. That is point is defined by what we understand to be ultimate truths (haqa'iq).[10]

Another major difference is that the first objective of transformative education is a form of self-awareness that makes the autonomy of the individual sacrosanct. This arrangement leaves no room for the autonomy and authority of Allah. More radical advocates of transformative education, such as Stephen Brookfield, wed it with other aspects of critical theory. For them the goal of transformative education would be, in the context of a critique of Islam, identifying and challenging the assumptions that place Allah at the center of a hegemonic system of life, and destroying the power dynamics that constitute knowledge in a way that oppresses

[9] *Ibid.*

[10] *I mention that this is true up to a point for at the level of spirituality and ethical behavior, the believer endeavors to ascend to ever higher degrees of human perfection. As we will never attain perfection, spiritually or ethically, if we remain on the path of spiritual refinement our "transformation" never ceases in this world.*

the individual.[11]

The knowledge brought by the Prophet ﷺ while transformative, emanates from an epistemic base that centers on Allah, His autonomy and His authority. Here, for Muslims, the goal of transformation is the subordination of the self. We read in the Qur'an, *As for one who fears when he will stand before his Lord and denies his soul its whims, Paradise will be his place of refuge.* (79:40) The Prophet ﷺ mentioned in a hadith, "No one of you truly believes until his whims are consistent with what I have brought."[12] Hence, the transformation encouraged through Islamic, indeed through prophetic education, is not one that sanctifies the individual, nor is it open-ended.

To accomplish the twin objectives I have alluded to in the above discussion: exalting Allah, and subordinating the individual self; inculcating humility into human consciousness was one of the focal points of the Prophet's teachings ﷺ. It is also one of the keys to real human liberation, as it allows for the freeing of the spirit (ruh), the unique aspect of our being, which coupled with the power of our intellect distinguishes us from the rest of creation. He mentioned in this regard, "Allah has revealed to me [to instruct] you to humble yourselves in order that no one exults over another, nor transgresses against him."[13] He also mentioned, "Charity will never decrease wealth. Allah will only increase a pardoning servant in honor. And no one humbles himself for the Sake of Allah except that Allah elevates him."[14]

---

[11] *See Mezirow, 125-150, for Brookfield's discussion of transformative learning as the basis for a critique of ideology.*

[12] *Nawawi, al-Arba'in, 41.*

[13] *Muslim, 2865.*

[14] *Muslim, 2588.*

When the human being is humble, the suppression of the ego (the soul in its unrefined state) is an easy matter. The state of humility allows one to glorify and sanctify Allah, to keep life in perspective, to strive for otherworldly salvation, to understand and respect knowledge that is not rooted in the frailties of human thought, and to enter upon the path to true human liberation –from the ego, Satan, the whims of the soul, and the seductiveness of the world.

To a large degree, these lessons are at the heart of the teachings our Prophet, Muhammad ﷺ. That he was able to convey them so effectively, as has been demonstrated by Shaykh Abu Ghuddah in this timely volume, is one of the secrets to the continued viability of Islam.

Imam Zaid Shakir
Zaytuna College, US

AUTHOR'S PREFACE

All praise is due to Allah Who taught by the pen; taught mankind that which they did not know. May salutations and peace be upon His Messenger and our leader, Muḥammad ﷺ, upon his family, his companions and those who follow them in good till the Day of Judgment.

These sublime words and blessed and noble traditions were originally a lecture that I gave at the request of the College of *Sharīʿa* and Arabic Language in Riyadh, Saudi Arabia during my first year of teaching there on the evening of Monday 17th Shawwāl 1385 AH, 7th February 1965.

I selected this topic "The Teacher-Messenger ﷺ and his methods of teaching" due to its profound connection with knowledge, scholars, teaching and students. In the years that passed, I have added many important and complementary topics with comments both long and short, as were needed to bring out this comprehensive book.

I did my best to make this book comprehensible for all its readers and to benefit the lay and the learned alike. This is a topic of great importance since it covers a very crucial aspect of the Teaching Prophet ﷺ and his noble life. It is a book of instruction, education and teaching for both the teacher and student.

The subject of this book is rare and unique. It is the culmination of over 30 years of research and no one, to my knowledge, has written on this topic in this manner before. I have waited this long period of time, continuously enhancing it with 'final' touches in an attempt to approach perfection. This desire to attain perfection has left many great works incomplete. Likewise, delay and procrastination have left incomplete many unique books. Since I announced that I will be publishing this book, I have received numerous requests from those who have heard about it to bring it out. Unfortunately, I was not able to fulfil their wishes earlier. Now, I praise Allah for His blessing and the great opportunity He has bestowed upon me. In the meantime, some esteemed colleagues followed my example with their own writings and research.

I have quoted many Prophetic narrations from the *Sunnah* [Prophetic example] of the Prophet ﷺ outlining his methods of teaching. I have divided this book into two parts. The first part covers the Prophet's ﷺ noble personality and traits and his wise actions. In the second part I have reviewed his teaching methods and his right guidance and directions. In my research I was keen to cite the noble aḥādīth that, apart from being descriptive and explanatory, are clearly educational in scope. These aḥādīth highlight educational and instructional examples under well-defined titles.

I have annotated the source of each ḥadīth. If I attribute it to one of the Six Narrators; Bukhārī, Muslim, Abū Dāwūd, an-Nasā'ī, Tirmidhī and Ibn Mājah, that means it is reported in their main work. If I have quoted a ḥadīth from other sources then I have provided full details.

Keep in mind that a single ḥadīth may cover more than one educational aspect or teaching method and therefore, could be quoted in more than one aspect. If I have quoted it only in one aspect, that should not be construed to confine it to that aspect alone.

I pray to Allah ﷻ the Generous, to bring benefit through this book and to accept it purely for His sake. I pray that it will be an incentive for my readers to follow the words and deeds of the Prophet ﷺ in all matters and under all circumstances. For surely that can only bring good, all good to us.

Allah ﷻ guides those who seek His guidance. He is our Lord and we have no Lord but Him, success is in His hands and He is able to do everything. All praise is due to Allah, the Lord of the universe. May greetings and peace be upon our leader Muḥammad ﷺ, his family and his companions.

Shaykh ʿAbd al-Fattāḥ Abū Ghuddah
Riyadh, 26 Muḥarram 1416 AH - 24 June 1995

TESTIMONY OF THE QUR'ĀN, SUNNA, & HISTORY

The Noble Qur'ān confirms the Messenger of Allah ﷺ as a teacher to people and to all of humanity despite being unlettered and hailing from a desert environment. Allah ﷻ says[1], "It is He who sent among the unlettered people a messenger from amongst themselves, reciting to them His verses, purifying them and teaching them the Book and the wisdom. Although, they were indeed before this in manifest error." Allah ﷻ says[2], "And We have sent you [O Prophet ﷺ] as a messenger unto all mankind and Allah is sufficient as a witness." Allah ﷻ also says[3], "We have not sent you [O Prophet ﷺ] except to the whole of mankind as a bearer of glad tidings and a warner; but most people do not know."

The purified *Sunnah* also confirms that the Messenger of Allah ﷺ is an insightful guide and teacher.

❖ ḤADĪTH **1**: Ad-Dārimī and Ibn Mājah, the wording is his reported[4] on the authority of ᶜAbdullah ibn ᶜAmr ibn al-ᶜĀṣ (may Allah be pleased with them both[5]) who said, 'One day the Messenger of Allah ﷺ exited from some of his rooms and entered the mosque and he was by two groups. One of them were reading the Qur'ān and supplicating to Allah, Exalted be He and the other group were learning and teaching and the Prophet ﷺ commented, "All are engaged in good, these are reading the Qur'ān and supplicating to Allah. If Allah wishes He will either grant them [what they ask for] or deny them. And these are teaching and learning and I have not been sent but as a teacher." Then he sat with them.'

Indeed Allah sent him as a teacher. This teacher and great educator, unrivalled in the history of humanity, was unlettered but insightful and a Prophet and a brilliant Messenger. To his teachings and guidance are indebted many nations, peoples and societies numbering hundreds of millions in all parts of the world. They venerate him, faithfully follow his guidance and seek the pleasure of Allah ﷻ through following and emulating him.

With kindness, he relentlessly educated the Arabs despite their rough nature, extreme rudeness and inconsistent characters. He withstood their rudeness and remained patient over their derision and harm. Ultimately, they accepted his call and rallied around his flag. For him and in his defence they sacrificed themselves and fought their dearest, fathers and relatives. In obedience of his orders, they abandoned loved ones, homeland, clans and brothers. All this was done solely for him who did not read and write or study the books of earlier peoples or previous educators. If we contemplate upon this we will come to the logical conclusion that he alone is the most important teacher, the Messenger of Allah, may Allah's peace and salutations be upon him.

Carlyle described the pre-Islamic conditions of the Arabs:

> The rest of the Nation, fractioned and cut asunder by deserts, lived under similar rude patriarchal governments by one or several: herdsmen, carriers, traders, generally robbers too; being oftenest at war one with another, or with all: held together by no open bond... In this way had the Arabs lived for long ages, unnoticed by the world; a people of great qualities, unconsciously waiting for the day when they should become notable to the entire world.

> It was as a birth from darkness into light; Arabia first became alive by means of it. A poor shepherd people, roaming unnoticed in its deserts since the creation of the world: a Hero-Prophet was sent down to them with a word they could believe: see, the unnoticed becomes world-notable, the small has grown world-great; within one century afterwards, Arabia is at Grenada on this hand, at Delhi on that; glancing in valour and splendour and the light of genius, Arabia shines through long ages over a great section of the world.'[6]

❖ ḤADĪTH 2: Muslim reported[7] in the 'Book of Divorce' from his *Ṣaḥīḥ*, the story when the Prophet ﷺ gave his noble wives (may Allah be pleased with all of them) the choice of remaining married to him or leaving. He started with ʿĀ'ishah from them and she (may Allah be pleased with her) opted to remain with him but asked him not to tell the others that she had chosen him. Then he ﷺ replied, "Indeed Allah did not send me to harm others or cause difficulty for them. Rather, He sent me as a teacher and to put people at ease."

Imām al-Ghazālī commented[8] on the Prophet's ﷺ indirect way of chastising ʿĀishah ﷺ noting that 'one of the intricacies of the educational process is to chastise the student for any misbehaviour indirectly and not blatantly. Overt reprimand shatters respect and leads to audacity and aggressive disagreement and causes insistence upon a wrong viewpoint.'

❖ ḤADĪTH 3: Muslim reported[9] also on the authority of Muʿāwiyah ibn al-Ḥakam as-Sulamī ﷺ who said, 'Whilst I was praying with the Messenger of Allah ﷺ, a person among the congregation sneezed. I said, 'May Allah have mercy upon you.' Then all the people starred at me with disapproving looks, so I said, 'May my mother lose me! Why are you staring at me?' Then they began slapping their thighs with their hands. When I saw them silencing me, I kept silent. When the Messenger of Allah ﷺ completed the prayer he called me. May my father and mother be his protection!

I have never seen a better teacher in his way of teaching before him or after him. For by Allah, he did not reproach me, hit me, or revile me. Then he said, "Ordinary talk of people does not befit this prayer. Only Allah's praise and glorification and recitation of the Qur'ān." Or the Messenger of Allah ﷺ said words to that effect.

We see the calmness and gentleness of the Prophet ﷺ in this ḥadīth when he told this companion that prayers should be devoted for the praise and glorification of Allah, recitation of the Qur'ān and supplication. He told him that ordinary speech is prohibited during prayers so he should not bless a person who sneezes, return greetings, or answer a question as all such acts would invalidate the prayer.

Imām an-Nawawī commented[10] on this ḥadīth, 'This ḥadīth portrays the great character of the Prophet ﷺ as Allah Himself testified. It illustrates his kindness to the ignorant, his compassion and mercy to his followers. This ḥadīth encourages us to follow his example in being kind to the ignorant and to teach him in an effective and gentle manner that will make him understand what is right."

History likewise testifies that the Messenger of Allah ﷺ was a teacher and what a great teacher he was! A cursory review of the state of humanity before the Messenger of Allah ﷺ and how it was transformed after his message will give us the clearest testimony and proof to this fact.

If we review exemplary human teachers that humanity has since seen after the Teacher-Messenger ﷺ, we will see the strongest proof of the magnificence of this great teacher and educator. The legacies of all other great personalities in the world of teaching and education pale into insignificance in comparison to his.

Was there another teacher who rivalled him in the quantity and quality of his graduates; the Companions and Successors? How were they before him and what transformation did they undergo through him? Every single one of the Companions is a walking proof of the greatness of this unique and unrivalled teacher and educator. This reminds us of a very sound statement of a scholar, who said, 'If the Messenger of Allah ﷺ had no miracle but his Companions, they would have been a sufficient proof of his prophethood.'[11]

It is not just a mere coincidence that such a vast number of people graduated at his ﷺ hands in such a short period of time. He ﷺ took them along an express path of collective education and pushed them hard to eradicate illiteracy. He encouraged, persuaded and warned them strongly against acquiescence to ignorance. They responded enthusiastically and came to learn and have a thorough understanding of the religion. They started teaching each others and learning from each other and became literate in a short span of time.

❖ ḤADĪTH 4: Al-Ḥāfiẓ al-Mundhirī reported[12] in his book *At-Targhīb wa-t-Tarhīb* in the Book of Knowledge on the authority of ʿAbdur Raḥmān ibn Abzā ﷺ who said, 'One day the Messenger of Allah ﷺ addressed [the people], he praised Allah and extolled Him. He then mentioned some groups of Muslims and praised them with goodness. Thereafter he said, "What is wrong with some people that they do not educate and teach their neighbours? Why do they not enlighten them? Why don't they command them [to the right] and prohibit them [from the wrong]?"

"Why don't some people learn from their neighbours? Why don't they seek knowledge or enlightenment? By Allah, people should teach, inform, enlighten, command and forbid their neighbours. People should learn, get knowledge and gain enlightenment from their neighbours. If not, I will surely be prompt to punish [them] in this life."

Then he came down and entered his home. Some people wondered, 'whom is he referring to?' They concluded, 'they are the Ashʿarites, a group of learned jurists with ill-mannered neighbours who dwell in the desert and around creeks.' The Ashʿarites heard the story and they came to the Messenger of Allah ﷺ and asked, 'O Messenger of Allah, you praised one group but disapproved of us. Why?'

He replied, "People should teach their neighbours! They should enlighten them and tell them the right and the wrong. People should learn from their neighbours. They should seek knowledge and enlightenment from their neighbours. If not, I will surely be prompt to punish [them] in this life."

They asked, 'O Messenger of Allah! Are we obliged to teach others?' The Messenger repeated his statement. They asked again, 'Are we obliged to teach others?' He answered the same. They then said, 'Give us one year.' And he gave them a respite of one year to educate, teach and enlighten their neighbours.

Then the Messenger of Allah ﷺ recited this verse[13], "The unbelievers among the Children of Israel were cursed by words of David and Jesus the son of Mary. This is because they disobeyed [God] and used to transgress. They would not forbid one another from an evil which they committed. How dreadful was what they used to do!"

We can infer a few lessons from this ḥadīth:

The Prophet ﷺ pointed out the duty of learned neighbours towards their less-learned. This is based on the rights of the Islamic brotherhood and that of neighbourly relationship. In Islam, the right of neighbours is almost as strong as that of kinship and inheritance. The Prophet ﷺ said, "Gabriel continued recommending to me the rights of the neighbour till I thought he would give him some inheritance.[14]" The Prophet ﷺ pointed out that a neighbour could be the closest to an inheritor just because he lives next to us. Neighbourhood can take several forms: one is living next to each other; another is belonging to the same mosque, school, neighbourhood, trade, etc... Inheritance is of two kinds: tangible, entailing the inheritance of wealth and intangible, entailing the inheritance of knowledge. It is the duty of every person to guide his neighbours to what they should do and what benefits them. Knowledge is most beneficial and hence tops the list of duties to be shown towards a neighbour. Peace and salutations of Allah be upon the teacher of good to mankind and the guide to all humanity.

Commenting on this ḥadīth, our respected teacher Muṣṭafā az-Zarqa in his book, The General Introduction to Fiqh, *al-Madkhal al-Fiqhī al-ʿĀm*, said[15], 'This great stand that stresses the sanctity of knowledge and regards laxity in teaching and learning a collective crime subject to penal punishment is unprecedented in history. Islam considers negligence of religious duties a punishable social evil and these duties include teaching and learning. If a scholar did not perform his duties of teaching or an ignorant person did not seek to learn the essentials prescribed by the religion, then both are liable to be punished due to their failure in complying with the following command of the Prophet ﷺ:'

❖ ḤADĪTH 5: Ibn Mājah reported[16] on the authority of Anas ؓ that the Prophet ﷺ said, "Seeking knowledge is a duty upon every Muslim."

I would like to add to his comments on this ḥadīth "Seeking knowledge is a duty upon every Muslim" that the Prophet ﷺ made seeking knowledge, regardless of gender, a condition to attain the full title of being a Muslim. Thus, he drew our attention to the belief that whoever claims to belong to Islam should seek and acquire knowledge. How can Islam tolerate ignorance when the first revelation of the Book of Allah was[17], "*Read in the name of your Lord Who has created. Created man from a clot. Read and your Lord is Most Kind, Who taught [man] by the pen - taught man what he did not know!*"

MANNERS & EDUCATIONAL SKILLS OF THE PROPHET

We would like to enjoy and benefit from this pioneering teacher and unlettered Prophet ﷺ all the aspects of his guidance, means and objectives. These few pages would not allow more than covering some of his methods in teaching and education. As for the major objectives of this great teacher, I pray that Allah ﷻ will enable me to cover these adequately on other occasions.

Allah ﷻ bestowed upon this teacher of goodness, despite being unlettered and unable to read or write, a unique knowledge among human beings. Allah complemented His blessings with a brilliant, comprehensive and unique personality. Allah ﷻ alluded to that in His saying[18], "... He taught you [O Prophet ﷺ] that which you did not know; And Allah's favour upon you was very great."

The Prophet ﷺ endeavoured to propagate and spread knowledge amongst people. He was indeed, the principal teacher of goodness in this world when we consider beauty of speech, eloquence of words, clarity of expression, smoothness of methods, subtlety of signals, radiating spirit, open heartedness, ample mercy, abundant compassion, wise forcefulness, great attention, superior intelligence, extreme concern and his tremendous kindness towards people. Thus, he ﷺ summarised his mission as, "I have only been sent as a teacher." Before delving into his teaching methods, I believe it is appropriate to mention a few words about how wary and cautioning this Noble Teacher was against useless knowledge. He included this among supplications that he often prayed,

❖ ḤADĪTH 6: Muslim reported[19] on the authority of Zayd ibn Arqam ﷺ who said, 'The Messenger of Allah ﷺ used to say, "O Allah! I indeed seek Your protection from a knowledge that carries no benefit, from a heart that is not humble, from a soul that does not feel contented and from a supplication that is not answered."'

The Prophet ﷺ was a teacher by his words as well as his deeds. These prayers are therefore a guidance from him to both the teacher and the student that they should learn or teach what is beneficial and consistent with the pure *Sharīʿa*.

The knowledge referred to here is that which would lead to harm whether to its seeker or to others, hence it is disapproved of because of its consequences. The means to an evil entails evil. Thus tricks and mischief that lead to corruption and the ability to trample over the rights of others are disliked, may Allah protect us from it. Knowledge and skills that enable a person to steal or embezzle the wealth of people without leaving a trace is, doubtlessly, evil knowledge that has no benefit. Being void of such knowledge is, ultimately, much better than mastering it. Certain types of knowledge can be detrimental to some people as, for example meat and sweets will harm an infant who is being breast-fed. Sometimes, ignorance of certain knowledge is bliss. Many have pursued knowledge they do not need and subsequently caused harm either to their spiritual or material life and suffered the worst loss of their most valuable asset – life itself! They could have utilized their time in a much better way. I pray to Allah ﷻ to guide us to what benefits us, to enable us to benefit from what He taught us and to keep us away from what is harmful to our religion or mode of living.

It is appropriate to cover some of the aspects of the Prophet's ﷺ personality as a teacher. Doing this will bring us closer to the noble soul which Allah blessed His Messenger with in order to bring good to the people and to convey the religion to the whole of mankind.

The Prophet ﷺ was of the highest rank and loftiest nature in his compassion and mercy. He shunned complexity and loved ease. He was kind and keen with students conveying knowledge and goodness to them at all times and all situations. Truly Allah ﷻ said[20], "Indeed there has come to you [O mankind] a messenger from amongst yourselves: it weighs heavily upon him what troubles you; [he is] keen over you and extremely compassionate and merciful to the believers."

❖ ḤADĪTH 7: Muslim and Bukhārī, the wording is his reported[21] and the wording is, on the authority of Mālik ibn al-Ḥuwayrith ﷺ, who said, 'We came to the Messenger of Allah ﷺ whilst we were a group of youth of similar age. We remained in his company for twenty days. The Messenger of Allah ﷺ was extremely merciful and compassionate. When he felt that we were home-sick, he asked us about those whom we left behind. We informed him and he told us, "Go back to your families and stay with them. Teach them and command them and pray as you have seen me pray. When prayers are due, one of you should make the call [to prayer] and the eldest should lead you."' This ḥadīth highlights several educational aspects:

An excellent example of a group of youth travelling to a scholar to learn and to understand their religion at his hand.

The youth, while remaining with the scholar for sometime, will observe his behaviour, guidance and practices. In remaining close to him for many days, their young and tender minds will gain an insightful understanding of his teachings and how to apply it in practice. This practical teaching left them with full awareness and better behaviour for the rest of their lives as the Companions of the Prophet ﷺ.

This ḥadīth indicates learning just by observing the Prophet's ﷺ personal traits that encompassed the best of examples and presented the perfect human being.

The rules of the *Sharīʿa* are learnt from the Prophet ﷺ.

It is recommended for the student to seek the most knowledgeable and insightful scholar of his time. The parents of these youths were also Companions of the Prophet; they met him and learned and gained knowledge from him. Yet the youths were not just content with learning from their parents. Rather they sought the leader of scholars, the crown of Prophets and the most learned of all mankind.

The Prophet ﷺ specified that the eldest should lead the prayers, since they were all equal in their knowledge and learning from him. As such, age becomes the factor of preference. If one of them was more knowledgeable, then he should be given preference as knowledge is the most distinguishing factor. I have covered the issue of ranking more extensively in my book entitled "Islamic Manners".

❖ ḤADĪTH 8: Imām at-Tirmidhī reported[22], in his book Prophetic Traits *'Shamā'il'*, on the authority of ʿĀ'ishah, who said, 'The Messenger of Allah ﷺ never used to speak without a pause as you do. Rather he used to speak a clear and distinct talk that could be memorized by the one sitting with him.'

❖ ḤADĪTH 9: Imām at-Tirmidhī reported[23] also in his book Prophetic Traits *'Shamā'il'*, on the authority of Anas ibn Mālik who said, 'The Messenger of Allah ﷺ used to repeat a word three times so that he is fully understood.'

It is clear from these two aḥādīth, that the Prophet ﷺ was

conducting himself as a skilful teacher who would talk slowly and clearly to avoid any confusion or misunderstanding. He used concise and focused sentences ensuring what he said was clearly understood and firmly embedded in the mind of the listeners. The Prophet ﷺ was motivated by his noble mission of guidance and compassion to his nation in general and to his students in particular. These noble aḥādīth indicate that the teacher should teach his students at a measured pace and focus upon covering the whole topic. Teachers should be prepared to repeat till they are clearly understood.

❖ ḤADĪTH **10**: Imām at-Tirmidhī reported[24], in his book Prophetic Traits *'Shamā'il'* on the authority of al-Ḥasan ibn ʿAlī (may Allah be pleased with both of them), who said, 'I asked my uncle, Hind ibn Abī Hālah, who enjoyed a descriptive memory of the Messenger of Allah ﷺ, to describe for me the speech of the Messenger of Allah ﷺ. He said, 'The Messenger of Allah ﷺ was in constant worry and always pensive. He never took full rest. He remained silent for long periods of time and spoke only when needed. He would start and conclude his speech with the name of Allah. His words were brief but laden with meanings. His speech was clear beyond misunderstanding and was neither too long nor too short.

He was not harsh yet could not be underestimated. He was highly appreciative of food as the bounty of Allah however minute - he never frowned at any. He did not disapprove of any food or drink nor did he praise it. He was never angered by worldly matters nor did it concern him. But if a right was trampled upon, his anger would not settle till it prevailed, though he was never angry or vengeful for anything personal.

When he pointed to something he used his entire palm. When he expressed wonder he turned his palm downside up. When he spoke, he struck the base of his left thumb with the palm of his right hand. If he became angry, he would turn away and would not look into the eyes. When pleased, he would lower his gaze. His laugh was mostly a smile. When he laughed, his teeth glittered like white hailstones."

That the Prophet ﷺ was in constant worry, does not mean, as the scholars have explained, that he was distressed about worldly gains or difficulties. He was never like that. What he was in constant worry and concern about were important matters like the call to Allah; attracting people towards it and convincing them to embrace it. In addition to this, he was continuously struggling with the polytheists, teaching the ignorant while at the same time worshipping Allah in the best manner. This is elaborated in the next sentence that described him as 'always pensive. He never took full rest; He remained silent for long periods of time.' However, one must not forget that this was when he was alone as he was cheerful when with others.

The words of the Prophet ﷺ were brief but laden with meanings. This is evident from many of his sayings like:

1. "The essence of religion is to give sincere advice." (Muslim)
2. "Observe Allah and He will protect you." (Tirmidhī, Aḥmad)
3. "Observe Allah wherever you are." (Tirmidhī, Aḥmad, Dāramī)
4. "The allowed *(ḥalāl)* is clear and the forbidden *(ḥarām)* is clear." (Bukhārī, Muslim)
5. "When you feel no shame, then do as you please." (Bukhārī)
6. "Leave what is doubtful to what is doubtless." (Tirmidhī, An-Nasā'ī, Aḥmad, Mustadrak)
7. "Allah has decreed excellence for every matter." (Muslim)
8. "Verily Allah, exalted is He, is pure and only accepts that which is pure." (Muslim)
9. "Hellfire is veiled with desires and Paradise is veiled with displeasures." (Bukhārī, Muslim, Tirmidhī)

10. "The [true] Muslim is he from whom Muslims feel safe from his tongue [words] and his hand [deeds]." (Bukhārī, Muslim)

11. "Of the excellence of one's Islam is that he leaves that which does not concern him." (Tirmidhī, Aḥmad)

12. "Deeds are based on intentions and every man has only that which he intended." (Bukhārī, Muslim)

13. "Verily Satan runs through a human like blood runs [through the body]." (Bukhārī)

14. "None of you will have attained perfect faith till he loves for his [Muslim] brother what he loves for himself." (Bukhārī, Muslim)

15. "Exercise abstinence from the world and Allah will love you, and abstain from what people have and they will love you." (Tirmidhī, Ibn Mājah, Mustadrak)

16. "That which I forbid you, avoid it, and that which I command you, do of it what you are able." (Bukhārī, Muslim)

17. "If people were to be given according to what they claim, men would claim people's property and blood, but clear evidence is required of a claimant and an oath is required of one who denies [the claim]." (Bayhaqī)

18. "Don't harm yourselves or harm others." (Ibn Mājah, ad-Dārqutnī)

19. "Righteousness is what your soul feels at ease with and your heart feels comfortable with. Evil is what your soul becomes agitated with and it goes agitatedly to and fro in the chest even though people repeatedly give you a judgement [as to a matter's permissibility." (Aḥmad, Dārimī)

20. "The best guidance is the guidance of Muḥammad ﷺ, the worst of issues are those [religious] innovations and every heresy is a clear falsehood." (Muslim)

21. "Whoever innovates something reprehensible in this matter of ours that does not belong to it is rejected." (Bukhārī, Muslim)[25]

The Prophet ﷺ was keen on important and humane issues. He was not an epicure. The topics of his talk had nothing to with admiring best foods or drinks as we see with some people who are taken with food, drink and other worldly pleasures and it constitutes the focus of their talks.

When a person angered the Prophet ﷺ he would not reciprocate with more anger. He would steer away from him.

To laugh when it is appropriate is a good trait since it fits with human instinct. No wonder that the Prophet ﷺ would laugh when facing a funny situation.

The great prolific Arab writer, al-Jāhiz, in the beginning of his book The Misers [*al-Bukhalā'*] spoke about the advantage of crying and its benefit to the body and the soul and then he said,

'Then imagine the benefit of laughing that keeps a person very happy. If laughing was a despised act whether by the originator or those responding to it, people would not describe as laughing flowers, dresses, jewellery, or mansions. Allah described himself, "It is He who brought laughter and crying and it is He who brought death and life." Thus, He put laughter parallel to life and crying parallel to death. Besides, Allah does not add a bad attribute to Himself or remind His creatures with a flaw.

Indeed, laughter is a great component of a happy personality and a very beneficial act. It is a basic instinct and distinctive part of the human creation. Laughter is the first pleasant act an infant does and with it happiness comes and good health and strength continues.

Arabs liked laughter and thus they called their children *Ḍaḥḥāk* Laughing, *Bassām* Smiling, *Talq* cheery *and Talīq* jovial. The Prophet ﷺ laughed and joked and likewise did pious forefathers. If the Arabs praised a person they would say, 'Laughing teeth, an evening smile, cheerful to his guest, generous and easygoing.' If they disparaged someone, they would say that he is 'grim-faced, frowning, dreadful appearance, stern, unsympathetic and a vinegar face.'

However, laughter should be appropriate in its timing and extent and joking should be appropriate in its timing and extent. In both if went above, or below, the norm you will be criticized for your faux pas. Useful jokes and appropriate laughter will lend you more seriousness and respect.'

❖ ḤADĪTH **11**: Imām Tirmidhī reported[26], in his book Prophetic Traits *'Shamā'il'* on the authority of al-Ḥasan ibn ʿAlī (may Allah be pleased with both of them) who said, al-Ḥusayn ibn ʿAlī said I asked my father ʿAlī ibn Abī Ṭālib ؓ about the Messenger of Allah's ﷺ manner with those in his company. He said, 'The Messenger of Allah ﷺ was always cheerful, easy-going and approachable. He was not stern or insensitive. He did not yell or use foul language. He did not seek the faults of others or over praise them. He ignored what he did not like and never left you hopeless of his generosity or turned you back empty handed.

He discarded three traits: squabbling, greed and curiosity. He spared people three traits: he did not criticize or condemn anyone. He did not search for faults and spoke only what he hoped Allah will reward him for.

When he spoke those present listened motionlessly with their heads lowered as if birds were upon them. Once he fell silent, they would talk. They would wait for their turn to speak in his presence and when a person talked, they remained silent till he finished. Whoever started talking will be listened to. The Prophet shared their laughter and wondered at their wonder.

He was tolerant towards the stranger in their coarse way of speaking and asking; so much so that his companions enticed them. He used to say, "If you see someone asking for a favour, be generous to them." He would not accept praise for no reason. He would not interrupt the talk of a person unless he exceeds limits and then the Prophet would interrupt him by a word or simply by standing up.'

This ḥadīth which describes the Prophet ﷺ as a cheerful, down to earth and approachable person is simply an elaboration of the words of Allah who told the Prophet ﷺ, "Had you been rough or hard-hearted they would have dispersed from around you."

This ḥadīth illustrates the Prophet's manners of speaking and his choice of words.

The ḥadīth gives us an insight into the behaviour of the Prophet with people. He was fair to them; he would not belittle them or over praise them. He would close an eye to what he did not like to avoid embarrassing his companions and to remain above trivial matters.

The Prophet was generous and disliked to return people empty-handed.

The Prophet respected the privacy of people and did not seek to expose their faults and weaknesses nor did he spy on them.

The Companions respected the Prophet and enjoyed his speech and paid full attention, without creating any distraction, to what he said. This is the appropriate manners with seniors and esteemed persons.

The Prophet directed his Companions to follow proper order in their talks and discussion. This order respected the right of everyone present to contribute to the ensuing dialogue without interference.

The Prophet was extremely sensitive not to offend those who come to him from the countryside with their less than civilized manners. His companions noticed that and noticed, also, that those Bedouins would ask questions that no one else was willing to ask. They started encouraging them to ask the Prophet so they can benefit from his answers to their plain questions. Anas ﷺ, the servant of the Prophet ﷺ, said[27], 'The Qur'ān forbade us to ask the Prophet about certain things, so we would be pleased when a wise Bedouin would come to the Prophet and asked him while we were listening.' Anas ﷺ here alluded to the Qur'ānic verse, "O you who believe do not ask about things that if revealed to you, would dismay you." Before its revelation, the Companions used to ask the Prophet ﷺ too many questions, some of them were unnecessary and subsequently they were limited to ask only what was necessary and beneficial.

Anas ﷺ said a 'wise Bedouin' because a wise person knows how to put his question effectively, politely and succinctly. A wise person knows how to ask further questions and seek elaboration to make the discourse more rich and interesting.

In this regard, Imām Ibn al-Qayyim said, 'The Companions used to bring to the Prophet's attention all questions and doubts and he would answer it in a way that would bring understanding and comfort to their hearts. Both his supporters and his foes asked the Prophet; his enemies seeking to embarrass him and his supporters for clarification, understanding and to increase their faith. He answered both whatever they asked except what he had no answer for like the Day of Judgment.'

❖ ḤADĪTH 12: Imām Tirmidhī reported,[28] in his book Prophetic Traits *'Shamā'il'* on the authority of our master ʿAlī ﷺ in his portrayal of the meetings of the Messenger of Allah ﷺ. He said, 'He would share his courtesy among those present; each would feel he is getting preferential treatment.'

The Prophet ﷺ was most humble to students, learners seeking knowledge and those slow in understanding.

❖ ḤADĪTH 13: Bukhārī in *al-Adab al-Mufrad*, Nasā'ī and Muslim[29], the text is his, reported on the authority of Abū Rifāʿah al-ʿAdawī ﷺ who said, 'I arrived while the Prophet ﷺ was in the mid of a speech. So I said, 'O Messenger of Allah, I am a stranger who has come with questions about his religion; I do not know anything about my religion.' The Messenger of Allah ﷺ turned towards me, halted his speech and came to me. He was brought a chair with iron legs, I believe. He said, 'The Messenger of Allah ﷺ sat down [on that chair] and began teaching me of what Allah had taught him. He then went back to his speech and completed it.'

In his commentary on *Ṣaḥīḥ* Muslim[30], Imām Nawawī listed a few points that could be learned from this ḥadīth:

'This ḥadīth demonstrates how the Prophet ﷺ dealt with Muslims with humbleness, kindness, compassion and friendliness.

It also directs the learner to use tactful words and manners when asking a scholar.

The ḥadīth also teaches us that the scholar should be prompt in answering the learner. It indicates that first things should be addressed first. As it appears, the learner has asked about faith and its fundamental tenets. The scholars are unanimous that when a person inquires about faith and how to become Muslim, he should be immediately answered and taught.

The ḥadīth indicates that the Prophet ﷺ sat on a chair to enable others to hear his words and to see his noble face. I would like to add another point: the ḥadīth shows that it is permissible for the teacher to sit on a chair while teaching and that he is not obliged to teach while standing.

❖ ḤADĪTH **14:** Bukhārī, Nasā'ī and Ibn Mājah[31] reported on the authority of Sharīk ibn Abī Namir that he heard Anas ibn Mālik ؓ saying, 'While we were sitting in the mosque, a man on a camel came in, seated his camel in the courtyard of the mosque and then tied it. Then he asked to them, 'Which of you is Muḥammad?' - whilst the Prophet ﷺ was reclining amongst them – 'This leaning fair person' we answered.

The man addressed the Prophet, 'O son of ʿAbdul Muṭṭalib!'

"Here I am listening" the Prophet ﷺ replied. Then the man said to him, 'O Muḥammad! I am going to ask you and I will be tough on you in my questions, so do not get angry with me.' "Ask whatever you want" the Prophet replied.

The man said, 'I ask you in the name of your Lord and the Lord of those who came before you, did Allah send you to all of the people?' "By Allah! Yes" the Prophet replied. The man continued, 'By Allah, did Allah command you that we should pray five prayers in the day and night?' "By Allah! Yes" the Prophet replied.

The man said, 'By Allah, did Allah command you that we should fast this month of the year?' The Prophet replied, "By Allah! Yes." The man said, 'By Allah, did Allah command you to take this charity from our rich and distribute it amongst our poor?' The Prophet ﷺ replied, "By Allah! Yes."

The man said, 'I believe in what you came with and I am the envoy of my people whom I left behind. My name is Ḍimām ibn Thaʿlabah, the ally of Banī Saʿd ibn Bakr."

Nasā'ī reported this ḥadīth on the authority of Abū Hurayrah and concluded it, 'When the man left, the Prophet ﷺ said, "He truly understood."'

This ḥadīth covers a few lessons:

The humbleness of the Prophet ﷺ who was sitting among his companions as one of them.

The leader may recline while among his followers.

The admirable tact of this man who prepared for his question by apologising to the Prophet for his directness. He began every question by asking the Prophet by Allah to be confident, beyond the slightest hint of doubt, about the truthfulness of the Prophet.

Once he asked all his questions and received all the answers, he announced his Islam and informed the Prophet ﷺ that he is the envoy of his people who will become Muslims as they concur with his conclusion that the Prophet ﷺ was indeed a Messenger of Allah. They have full trust in his intelligence, thoughtfulness and far-sightedness. What an excellent people who sent such an excellent emissary.

For this ʿAbdullah ibn ʿAbbās ﷺ said, 'We never heard of an emissary better than Ḍimām.' ʿUmar ﷺ, used to say, 'I never saw anyone better than Ḍimām ibn Thaʿlabah in asking questions and being brief and precise.' May Allah be pleased with him.

❖ ḤADĪTH 15: Muslim[32] reported on the authority of Abū Ayyūb ﷺ that, 'A Bedouin approached the Messenger of Allah ﷺ whilst he was travelling and held the harness of the Prophet's camel. The Bedouin then said either, 'O Messenger of Allah!' or 'O Muḥammad!' 'Tell me what will bring me closer to paradise and distance me from hell.'

The Prophet ﷺ remained silent for a while, looked to his companions and then said, "He has certainly been blessed or guided." The Prophet ﷺ asked him, "How did you put it?" And the Bedouin repeated his question. Then The Prophet ﷺ replied, "Worship Allah and do not ascribe any partners with Him, establish prayers, give charity and maintain good relationships with your kith and kin. Let go of the camel!"'

This ḥadīth shows the Prophet's ﷺ humility and compassion with any enquirer even those who asked questions with the wrong manners or at the wrong time.

The Prophet ﷺ admired the appropriateness of the question and showed his admiration by asking him to repeat it. Then he told his companions about it.

The Bedouin held the harness of the camel practically holding the Prophet ﷺ while posing his question and getting his answer. The Prophet ﷺ patiently waited till the Bedouin got his reply and then asked him to let go.

❖ ḤADĪTH 16: Ibn as-Sakan, at-Ṭabarānī in his Large Collection *al-Muᶜjam al-Kabīr* and Abū Muslim al-Kajjī in his ḥadīth Collection *Sunan* reported on the authority of al-Mughīrah ibn ᶜAbdullah al-Yashkurī that his father told him, 'I went to Kūfah and entered the mosque where a man from the tribe of Qays called Ibn al-Muntafiq, was saying that, 'the Messenger of Allah ﷺ was described to me so I went looking for him till I met him at 'Arafat and pressed forward to talk to him. I was told 'Stay away from him.' But he said, "Let him come. He probably needs something." I therefore pressed forward until I reached him and took the harness of his camel and he did not get angry.'

I then said, 'Two things I shall ask you about. What will save me from the Hellfire? And what will get me into Paradise?' He looked to the sky and then turned to me with his noble face and said, "You have asked brief questions but the answers are very serious and long. Then understand this well: Worship Allah and do not ascribe anything to Him. Establish the mandatory prayers, give the required charity and fast the month of Ramadan."'

Again this ḥadīth demonstrates the Prophet's ﷺ humility and kindness to those who came to him with questions. He remained calm and put this man at ease with his questions and more importantly, with the answers.

❖ ḤADĪTH 17: Abū Dāwūd, Tirmidhī in Prophetic Traits *Shamā'il* and Muslim, the text is his, reported[33] on the authority of Anas ؓ that 'A mentally unstable woman said, 'O Messenger of Allah! I need you for something.' "O Lady! Choose any street you like until I get you what you want" he replied. He met her alone in a street till she finished telling him what she needed.' Abū Dāwūd in his version mentioned, 'She sat down and the Prophet ﷺ also sat down with her till she finished telling him what she needed.'

In his commentary to this ḥadīth, Imām Nawawī[34] said, 'This ḥadīth demonstrates the Prophet's humbleness. He stopped to address the need of a helpless woman and to respond, with confidentiality, to her request. However, this meeting should not be construed to bend the prohibition of meeting a strange woman alone because this was in a public road where passers-by would see them but could not hear them, thus maintaining the privacy of the poor woman.'

The Prophet's traits & personality

It is of paramount importance to review certain aspects of the traits of the Prophet ﷺ and his personality, since its review and understanding complement the understanding of his teaching role. Likewise, this is an indivisible part of his personality and mission. This review will help us to appreciate the font of his sayings and rulings and the importance of following his guidance in all aspects.

To illustrate this, I opted to summarize the words of the great Imām Abū al-Ḥasan Mawaradī (364-450 AH), Master of Judges, said in his book The Features of Prophet-hood *'Alam an-Nubuwwah*. The words of the Imām are full of guidance to what the teacher should follow in his behaviour, thinking, manners, work, ethics, style, appearance and sincerity. Remember that Allah said in the Qur'ān, "You have a fine example in the Messenger of Allah".

'The Prophets of Allah were the chosen amongst His servants and the best among his people, to fit the task he assigned to them. He brought them from the noblest elements and supported them with the strongest support to keep them free from any blemish in their lineage or performance. This will let people concede more easily to them and greatly increase admiration in them. Thus, people will be more prompt and obedient in responding to their call.

When we look at the Prophet ﷺ we see glaring genuine signs and encounter irrefutable proof that indeed he was the Prophet of

Allah. This is so obvious in his life from its beginning to its end. You can not discern any mixture of lies and truth or falsehood with facts. Allah sent him after purifying him to make him an object of admiration above any doubts. Logic would not refute him, hearts will embrace him and souls were attracted to him. He was prepared with the most honourable manners and best of deeds as solid foundations for his magnificent position as a Prophet or, if you will, an envoy of Allah among His creatures. His task was to look after their interests in obeying the Creator.

He was the perfect ambassador, for in his time there was no one even near to his stature, good nature or perfect manners and deeds. It is certainly not in vain that Allah described him in the Qur'ān, "Verily you [O Prophet ﷺ] are indeed upon the highest of manners."

Honour is not a miracle of Prophets; many ordinary people are honourable, but it is definitely a requirement. That a person is totally honourable is almost a miracle. Complete honour implies honesty which, in turn implies truthfulness.

Human perfection comprises four aspects, namely: appearance, behaviour, sayings and deeds. All four aspects were fully manifested in the Prophet ﷺ.

When we come to the first we find that, beside his fair appearance, the Prophet's ﷺ nature had four additional merits:

A simple presence that brought respect and awe and called for belief and submission. This occurred to people who were used to the Persian Imperial court and its pomposity. They were struck once they were in his presence though he did not seek this, for he was very modest and simple at heart.

Cheerfulness and positive attitudes that endeared him to people. None of his Companions hated or deserted him. They all liked him more than their own parents and children.

The Prophet ﷺ was well received by those around him and easily won the open hearts of those who met him and soon they were heeding his commands and looking to his guidance. No one abandoned him except those who were blinded by dislike and filled with envy.

People were keen to follow him and agreed with his decisions and were also willing to endure hardship and face adversity to implement it. None wavered and they remained loyal and faithful.

When we look at the behaviour of the Prophet ﷺ we notice six distinct traits:

Effective thinking, deep insight and correct reasoning. He was never conned by a trick, or gave-up in a difficulty. To the contrary, he would foresee ends at their beginnings.

He was calm despite being hunted and steadfast against hardship. He never feared troubles or broke down under the heaviest burden. He suffered at the hands of the Quraysh in Mecca the harshest of treatments but continued advocating his call feeling that victory will be, ultimately, his.

He was disinterested in amassing wealth and content with the bare necessities of life. Pleasure never captured his mind or guided his actions. He was the ruler of all of Arabia but shunned fortune and wealth. He died without leaving anything of value. He did not build a palace or a monument. He left his heirs nothing in order to steer them away from worldly possessions as he did. Any person who lived such an austere life is not to be thought for a moment to have been after wealth or riches. If he lied about Allah and falsely claimed his religion, he would not live on the minimum and leave the available for the sake of the Hereafter.

His modesty and humbleness with his followers. He walked around in the streets, sat on the ground and could not be distinguished from his followers except with his pensiveness and shyness.

This made him more respected and honoured. A Bedouin visited him and became nervous in his presence. He calmed him down and said to him, "Calm down. I am just the son of a woman who used to eat dried meat in Mecca."[35] He wanted the Bedouin, who perceived him like a king, to think of him as an ordinary human. He reminded the trembling man that he is the son of a woman, not a man who ate dried, not fresh meat - the food of the poor. This is all because of his noble nature and generous attitude. It is an original and genuine instinct without pretence or posturing.

He enjoyed a serene mind that would not respond unwisely to provocations. He would not argue or litigate beyond wisdom or logic. He dealt with rough Bedouins time after time and always kept his cool and never responded in anger or revenge. Allah protected him of all personal sways to remain always kind and merciful to people. The tribe of Quraysh, its noble and common people, opposed him with its entire means and attacked him with all kinds of attacks, but he remained patient and forgiving. The stronger their attacks were, the more forgiving he was. Even when he conquered them he held his wrath and forgave them. He asked them when he conquered Mecca, "What do you reckon I am going to do to you?" They replied, 'A kind cousin; if you forgive it is not unexpected. If you punish, we did wrong.' He said, "But I shall say like Yūsuf said to his brothers, 'No harm will reach today. May Allah forgive you and He is the Most Merciful.[36]'" Hind bint ʿUtbah who mutilated the liver of his uncle Ḥamzah ﷺ, came to him and he forgave her and accepted her as a believer. He fulfilled his pledges and kept his promises. He considered trickery a sin and breaking promises a dishonour. He kept his word regardless of difficulties or costs until his counterparts broke their agreement like Banū Qurayẓah and Banū an-Naḍīr and Quraysh when they broke the truce of al-Ḥudaybiyah, whereupon Allah brought good for him out of that.

Regarding his transcendent sayings we can discern eight traits:

His great wisdom and far-reaching knowledge despite being an unlettered person from an illiterate people; he never read a book, studied a science, or accompanied a scholar or a teacher. He came with what dazzled the minds and amazed the thoughts with its excellence and eloquence.

His grasp of what Allah revealed to him of the stories of the ancient Prophets with their people. He narrated it wholly without having it in a book or reviewing it with an expert. This stemmed from a superb mind, a learning soul and a big heart; three requisites for Prophets.

Supporting his teachings with clear evidence and explaining it with lucid rationalization. His words were easily understood and his reasoning was readily accepted. He said, "I have been endowed with saying so much with few words[37]" and indeed he was brief yet elaborate and concise yet detailed. This could come only with the help and guidance of Allah.

He enjoined fine manners and called for favoured behaviour. He prompted people to help their kin and to be compassionate with the weak and the orphans. He forbade envy and hatred and disliked breaking social relationships. He wanted his followers to be honourable, well mannered, well disposed to good deeds and to shun evil. As such, they met the description of Allah, "You have been the best nation sent to human kind; you enjoin the good and forbid the evil."[38] His followers followed his directions and heeded his warnings and with that they achieved success in this life and the hereafter. They became pious leaders and honest guides who brought strength to Islam and defeat to polytheism.

His clear answers to questions and supreme logic in arguments. Never in loss of words or incapable of explanation. He always won debates with clarity and reason.

He did not distort a saying or exaggerated a story reaching the borders of lying; he was known for truthfulness and trustworthiness in his youth and later to the extent that he was labelled with it. Before prophecy, Quraysh recognised these noble qualities, but they denied his prophecy out of envy, stubbornness, or just to discount him. If they could have proved that he had lied even once they would have presented that as an evidence of him telling falsehood. He who adhered to telling the truth whilst still young would not abandon it when old. He who did not lie to promote himself would not lie to promote Allah's teachings.

He would tailor his words according to need. He was neither shy nor talkative. Beyond that his respectful silence complemented his character. This explains why his sayings were memorised without distortion and pleasantly recalled and cited.

He was eloquent without using unfamiliar words or complex sentences. His style was simple but inimitable; if mixed with other sayings the disparities would clearly standout. Thus the authenticity of his sayings was greatly enhanced. The Prophet ﷺ was not known for literary talents or to be associated with speakers, poets or articulate people. The quality of his speech was original and nor acquired; Allah provided him what he needed for his task.

When we look at his noble deeds we can discern eight qualities:

His excellent conduct and way of life in bringing a religion that transformed people from their habitual creed and behaviour to a novel way of life and worship. Souls embraced his call and heeded his warnings; not an easy accomplishment unless one is backed by Allah and strengthened with a strong will. If he was implementing the orders of his Lord, then indeed that is an unequalled miracle. If it was his own endeavour, then it constitutes the ultimate proof. One marvels that the foundation he laid remained strong and attractive despite the passage of time and the change in the circumstances - a proof beyond proof.

In his conduct, he was able to combine the support of those who naturally leaned towards him and those who just accepted his authority. Both rallied under his flag and defended his message hoping for rewards or fearing punishment in this life or the hereafter. Both motives are always present due to the difference in nature and attitude amongst people and both are essential for success of religion and stability of life.

In his call, he advocated moderation not extremism. Exceeding reasonability is unwise and unsustainable.

He did not enjoin his followers to indulge in the worldly pleasures or to refuse it. He led them in a fair course in life. He guided them, "The best among you is the one who did not abandon his worldly life for his hereafter or his hereafter for his worldly life; the best of you is the one who takes from this and this [i.e. both].[39]" Indeed, devotion to one causes disorder and combing both is moderation. He also said, "Earthly life is a good vehicle if you ride it for the hereafter.[40]" That is because from it one takes supplies and accumulates credit with worship for the eternal life.

He detailed the laws of his religion and tackled novel issues, so much so that his followers had no ambiguity about the duties of worship or what is permissible and forbidden in contracts, marriages or other dealings. This led the People of the Book to adopt some of his laws for many issues that they themselves faced. His laws did not need to borrow from others. He laid for his laws rules that would facilitate the issuance of coherent and rational judgments on novel issues that may occur after divine revelation had ceased, avoiding confusion and meandering.

He ordered those present who learned from him to tell those absent to ensure that his teachings reached everyone. He commanded them, "Propagate but don't lie; others might be more insightful than those who have heard and sometimes you carry a ruling to those who understand it better than you.[41]" He faithfully accomplished his mission without leaving any gap in his duties towards his Lord or his followers. He did this in an unusually short period for such a daunting task- again a sign of divine guidance and support.

His life was a constant struggle with relentless enemies who attacked and besieged him while he was among a smaller number of strangers. He was able to turn this into victory and strength. His enemies feared him and dreaded his encounter. Thus, he combined calling to Allah and fending off his opponents; tasks unachievable except with the guidance and the support of Allah- a miracle for those who reflect.

His bravery in battles and steadfastness in encounters. Many times a battle would turn to the worse and he remained resolute and confident of victory or a draw. He never retreated or ran away. In the battle of Ḥunayn, his followers backed away and only nine companions remained around him. He was riding on a mule that could not outrun stallions and despite that he did not hesitate to reveal his place by calling out his companions, "Rally around me O servant of Allah! Truly I am the Prophet; the son of ʿAbdul Muṭṭalib!" They returned upon hearing his voice while his enemies didn't dare to approach him.

He never feared the numerous armies of his enemies or drew back in front of those attacking him. His courage was unrivalled; a caller told the inhabitants of Medina of an approaching attack and when they rushed to defend the city they found the Prophet coming from the other direction on saddle-less horse saying to them "don't worry." He had rushed ahead of everyone to explore the source of the threat and found it harmless.

This bravery is based on his full confidence that Allah will favour him with victory and his religion will spread through the whole earth. He said "Allah shrank the earth to enable me to see the east and the west. My nation will reach what I was shown."

His generosity and charitable nature. He gave everything and never retained anything. He lived poor and died with his shield pawned with a Jew. He became the sovereign of the Arabian Peninsula and controlled treasures and immense wealth but did not keep a Dirham or a Dinar for himself. In the battle of Hawazen he captured six thousand prisoners, twenty four thousands camels, forty thousands sheep and four thousand pounds of silver – he gave up all that was his and nothing remained in his hands.

ʿĀ'ishah ﷺ said, 'The Prophet did not leave a Dīnār or a Dirham, a sheep or a camel and he did not even leave a will." Abū Dharr narrated that the Prophet ﷺ said, "I would not be pleased if I have gold as much as the mountain of Uḥud and I spent it in the sake of Allah but kept one Dīnār on the eve of my death – except to pay a debt." If a person asked him a grant and he had nothing, he would ask him to buy what he wants and the Prophet ﷺ would pay the vendor later.

ʿUmar ibn al-Khaṭṭāb ﷺ said a man came to the Prophet ﷺ seeking for a grant and the Prophet said, "I have nothing but buy what you want and I shall pay that later." ʿUmar ﷺ said, "O Prophet of Allah, you gave him but Allah did not oblige you to exceed your means." The Prophet ﷺ disliked what ʿUmar ﷺ said and a man from the Anṣār said, "O Prophet of Allah! Give and fear not that your Lord will not give you." The Prophet ﷺ smiled and his face was lit, then he said, "This is what I was told to do." He used to say, "My responsibility towards the believers goes beyond their own personal responsibility. If a believer died leaving a debt; I shall pay it. Any believer leaving unfit heirs should come to me and

I shall look after them. Any believer leaving money it should go to his inheritors."

Where one can find such generosity or ascetic nature? No one could be his equal in this regard and even his enemies grudgingly acknowledged his generous character. The non-believers and the hypocrites were hunting for his mistakes and monitoring his behaviour. Were able to embellish him they would have not hesitated.

With these traits and behaviour he was qualified to lead his people and guide his followers. The duties of the message and of the leadership did not overwhelm him; he managed both in the best of ways accomplishing his divine tasks. Why? Because Allah created and nurtured him for this great accomplishment.

THE PROPHETIC METHOD OF TEACHING

After this indispensable review of the character of the Prophet we can resume illustrating his teaching methods.

In his teaching, the Prophet ﷺ selected methods that are most attractive, best suited and very effective with listeners as it matched their understanding and intellectual level. He used methods that helped them remember and memorize what he has said and facilitated their clear understanding of the issues in question.

The careful review of the collections of the Sunnah would show that the Prophet ﷺ used to employ different styles when speaking to his companions. At times, he would ask a question and at others, he would answer a question. Sometimes, he would answer just the question without elaboration while on other occasions, he would elaborate his answer. Sometimes, he would give an example to illustrate what he wanted to teach, at other times he would stress his message by taking an oath in Allah's name and, occasionally, he would bypass the answer if he deemed it wise. He taught, as the occasion merited, by writing, by drawing, or by citing a parallel. Sometimes he would be explicit and at others he will allude or insinuate.

At certain times, the Prophet ﷺ used to present a doubt only to dispel it with his answer. Sometimes, he would use jokes or reasoning to highlight the relevant points. Before touching upon a subject, he would prepare his listeners with a subtle and appropriate introduction. Many times he would compare things, while on other occasions he would point out the underlying reasons in the answers. He would solicit answers from his Companions, despite knowing the answer himself, in order to assess their knowledge. He would ask them in order to train them on how to find the answers by themselves. At times he would teach them even though they did not request.

He dedicated some of his lessons specifically for women and taught them whatever knowledge they needed. He was considerate to children and youngsters who were present. He would approach their teaching with a simpler ways that suited their innocence and playful nature.

These are some of the methods that I will illustrate in this book through quotations and stories from the books of Sunnah and biography of the Prophet ﷺ.

Teaching by his beautiful ways and character

The most important and significant method of the Prophet in teaching was his actions and exemplary behaviour; when he gave a command he would be the first to apply it. People would follow his example and emulate what they saw him do. His character exemplified the Qur'ān and as such he attained the highest of character and Allah made him a beautiful example for his servants. Allah said,[42] "There is for you in the Messenger of Allah a good example for those who seek Allah and the latter day and mention Allah abundantly." The Prophet ﷺ is therefore a role model for his followers in his character, his deeds and in all his affairs.

Teaching with practice is, undoubtedly, is the most effective and long lasting method. It helps understanding and remembering topics and it is most likely to be followed and emulated compared to plain words and rationalization. Learners instinctively like practical examples and this was the most distinguished and greatest teaching methods of the Prophet.

In his book, Splendid Review of the Islamic Jurisprudence *al-Fikr al-Sami fī Tārikh al-Fiqh al-Islamī,* the great Moroccan scholar Mohammad ibn Al-Husain al-Hajwi (1874-1956) said: "A proof that practice is more effective explanation than a verbal one is the action of the Prophet after signing the peace treaty of al-Hudaibia with Quraysh. The Prophet ordered his companions to come out of their *iḥrām* and to slaughter their sacrificial animals. He told them: 'Go and slaughter [your animals] and then shave off your heads.' They were reluctant to follow this order as they were not pleased with the treaty and were inclined to fight Quraysh. When the Prophet went into the tent of his wife Umm Salama and told her how the people were reluctant, she advised him to shave his own head and slaughter his sacrifice since the companions will inevitably follow him. He followed her advice and when they saw him they started slaughtering their animals and shaving the hair of each others despite their sadness. This demonstrates the high wisdom of Umm Salama as she reckoned that they have found it very difficult to do this while they have not accomplished their worship and that practical example speaks louder than words as the case was."[43]

The contemporaries of the Prophet did not miss this trait. al-Ḥāfiẓ Ibn Ḥajar in his collection of biographies of the companions, The Right Guide to Discerning the Companions *al-ʿIsabah fi Tamyiz al-Saḥāba,* reported on the authority of Ibn Isḥāq that the Prophet sent ʿAmr ibn al-ʿĀṣ to the great companion al-Julanda, the King of Oman, inviting him to Islam. Al-Julanda He said the following: "What convinced me about the truthfulness of this illiterate Prophet is that he does not command any good without being the first one to act on it. He does not forbid any evil without being the first one to abstain from it. When he conquers he remains humble and when he is overcome he does not become Abūsive. He keeps his word and fulfils his promises. I bear testimony that he is a Prophet."

In his book, *The Adherence* [*al-Iʿtiṣām*], Imām al-Shāṭibī (d. 790/1388) said: "The personality of the Prophet was an embodiment of the Qur'ān, because all his thoughts and deeds conformed with the divine revelation; he embraced it, propagated it, submitted to it, obeyed it and complied with its rulings."

This particular aspect was one of the strongest proofs of the truthfulness of his message. He enjoined but after he himself applying it first. He forbade and he was the first to cease. He admonished but addressed himself first. He wanted and was the first to heed. He brought hope and was most hopeful. The essence of all of this was adhering to the guidelines of the *Sharīʿa* to direct him to the straight path which he trod."

Because of this he became truly "a servant of Allah", which is the most honourable title a person can take. Allah said: "Exalted is He who took his servant by night..."[44], "Exalted is He who revealed the Criterion upon his servant."[45], "If you are in doubt regarding what We revealed upon Our servant."[46] And other similar verses wherein the Prophet is praised while described as the servant of Allah."

Based on that, all people should seek the *Sharīʿa* as their strict guidelines and a lighthouse to guide them to the right. They will be honoured proportionately to following its rules and applying it by words, belief and deeds. This is the highest rank of honour and it comes ahead of intellect or status, because Allah based honour on piety alone when He said: "Truly, the most honourable of you in the sight of Allah are those of you who are the most pious."[47] And whoever is more observant of this particular honour is the most deserving of honour. Whoever is not on par will not attain an honour similar to following the *Sharīʿa*. Indeed, honour commensurate with as much as we submit to the rules of *Sharīʿa*."[48]

As this method is the most distinct and most frequent among his methods of teachings, I shall quote here a few examples that demonstrate how he used this method in his teachings. There is no way to exhaustively cite them all here.

❖ ḤADĪTH **18**: Abū Dāwūd and Muslim, the text is his reported[49] on the authority of Jābir ibn ʿAbdullah ﷺ who said, 'The Messenger of Allah ﷺ joined us in this our mosque carrying in his hand a small branch from the palm trees of Ibn Tāb. He noticed some mucus on the front wall of the mosque so he scraped it off with that branch. He then came to us and said, "Who would like Allah to turn away from him?" We bowed our heads looking to the ground and the he asked again, "Who would like Allah to turn away from him?" Again, we bowed our heads looking to the ground. He asked again, "Who would like Allah to turn away from him?" We replied, 'None of us would like that O Messenger of Allah!'

He said, "When one of you stands up to pray, Allah is in front of him and therefore he should neither spit in front of him nor to his right. He could spit to his left under his left foot. If a cough overcomes you then do like this with your dress." And the Prophet wiped his mouth with the side of his dress.

The Prophet then said, "Get me a paste of perfume." A young boy from the neighbourhood rushed to his house and brought some in his palm. The Prophet took it and put it on the tip of the branch and swiped away the traces of the sputum.'

Jābir ﷺ commented, 'Therefore from this you began applying scented cream at your mosques."

That the Prophet ﷺ spoke about Allah being in front of a praying person is a metaphor that should not to be taken literally. We say about mosques that they are the houses of Allah and about the Kaʿbah that it is the Kaʿbah of Allah. This is a common literary usage to emphasize honouring and respecting these places. For example, Allah spoke in the Qur'ān about Prophet Ṣāliḥ ﷺ and the she-camel as the "She-camel of Allah."

Spitting was acceptable if one was overwhelmed during prayers in the mosque and if the floor of the mosque was either of sand, soil, or gravel as mosques were in the era of the Prophet. If the floor of the mosque is tiled, painted or carpeted as is the case with contemporary mosques, then one, if he has to do so, should wipe the sputum into his clothing, a tissue or handkerchief. Mosques should remain free of dirt and litter that would cause it to look dirty. Imām Bukhārī set an example of this in the following story cited by Ḥāfiẓ Ibn Ḥajar in his commentary on *Ṣaḥīḥ* al-Bukhārī[50].

"Muḥammad ibn Mansūr said we were gathered around Imām Bukhārī when a person took a shard off his beard and threw it to the floor of the mosque. Bukhārī noticed it and start watching people around him, when he felt no one was watching he took the shard and put it in his pocket. When he left the mosque he threw it in the street."

May Allah bless Imām Bukhārī how keen he was on keeping the mosque clean of a shard that a beard should be free of. May Allah bless him how tactful he was in accomplishing this.

The Prophet ﷺ repeated his words three times to make the message completely absorbed by those present.

Deeds are more effective in delivering the message and fully explaining its intent and extent.

The great humbleness of the Prophet ﷺ who personally scraped off the mucus.

Evil deeds should be denounced verbally.

Evil deeds should be remedied by counter deeds whenever possible.

In addition, this ḥadīth contains other social and fiqh lessons and benefits. It is mandatory to remove dirt and litter from mosques.Respecting mosques and keeping it free from any unsightly matter and litter.

Spit, mucus and phlegm are pure despite our natural repugnance. This is attested when the Prophet spat into his clothing to show them what a person should do when he is overcome by a sputum. Spitting and clearing throat does not void prayer provided that one does not utter more than two letters, or he is overwhelmed by spitting or mucus in his throat.

Out of respect for the direction of the *qiblah,* if a person has to spit, he should do so to his left side. He should not spit in front of him out of respect for the *qiblah* nor to his right side out of respect for the right even if he was not praying. One should spit to his left side as long as nothing prevents him from that. Muʿādh ibn Jabal ﷺ said, "I never spat to my right ever since I became Muslim."

The *Sharīʿa* is the basis of considering whether a conduct is good or bad. The right side is considered superior to the left and the hand is considered superior to the leg and Friday has virtue over other days.

Motivation to do as many good deeds as possible even if one already has done many. Ponder that the Prophet ﷺ, the leader of Prophets and righteous ones, personally scraped off the mucus.

Perfuming mosques is a Sunnah.

The ruler of Muslims should inspect mosques and ensure it is in good condition. Mosques deserve the inspection and the attention the leader of the believers as it is where Muslims gather and assemble, worship, learn, meet and consult and seek advice. Mosques are where Muslims have their command centres established and armies set forth for *jihād*. It is where Muslims go to meet their brothers and where their hearts and souls are attracted and the places where they meet delegations that come to meet them. So how much more they deserve to be inspected and paid attention to?

❖ ḤADĪTH 19: Tirmidhī, Nasā'ī, Ibn Mājah and Muslim, the text is his reported[51] on the authority of Sulaymān ibn Buraydah ibn al-Husayb al-Aslamī who heard his father saying that a man asked the Prophet ﷺ about the prayer times. He replied, "Pray with us for these two days." So when the sun passed noon, the Prophet ﷺ ordered Bilāl ؓ to call the Adhān and then ordered him to call the *Iqāmah* for Ẓuhr. Later he ordered him to establish the ʿAṣr prayer when the sun was quite high and brightly white. Then he ordered him establish the Maghrib prayer when the sun had just set. He then ordered him to establish the ʿIshā' prayer when the redness disappeared from the horizon. Later he ordered him to establish the Fajr prayer at the break of dawn.

When it was the second day, the Prophet ordered Bilāl to call the Ṭuhr prayer at a later time when it was comfortable and cool. He prayed ʿṣr when the sun was still high but he delayed more than the previous day. He prayed Maghrib just before the twilight disappeared. He prayed ʿIshā' when one third of the night had passed. He prayed Fajr when the sky was completely white.

Then the Prophet said, "Where is the one who asked about the prayer times?" The man replied, "Me, O Prophet of Allah!" the Prophet said, "The times of your prayers are in between what you saw."

The Prophet in this instance asked the enquirer to stay with him to learn the times of prayers in a practical way. Imām Nawawī, in his commentary on *Ṣaḥīḥ* Muslim said, "The ḥadīth indicated that explanation by practice is more effective in instruction. Practical explanations extend benefits beyond the enquirer to those present. The ḥadīth also indicates that an explanation could be delayed till when it is needed, which is the opinion of the majority of scholars of Principles of Fiqh."

❖ ḤADĪTH **20:** Nasā'ī, Ibn Mājah and Abū Dāwūd, the text is his reported[52] from the ḥadīth of ʿAmr ibn Shuʿayb through his father and his grandfather that a man came to the Prophet ﷺ and asked, 'O Prophet of Allah! How do I do ablution?'

Then the Messenger of Allah ﷺ called for water in a container and then washed his palms three times, his face three times and then his arms three times. He then passed his wet hands over his head, inserted his index fingers into his ears, passed his wet thumbs over the back of his ear lobes while his index fingers still inside his ear lobes. Then he washed his feet three times. He then said, "This is how ablution is done. Whoever does more or any less than this he has done harm and transgressed." Or [the narrator was not sure] "he has transgressed and done harm."

❖ ḤADĪTH **21:** Bukhārī reported[53] on the authority of Muʿādh ibn ʿAbdul Raḥmān that Ibn Abān told him saying, 'I brought ablution water to ʿUthmān ibn ʿAffān ﷺ whilst he was sitting on a seat. He then carried out his ablution in an excellent manner. He then said, 'I saw the Prophet ﷺ performing his ablution whilst sitting in this very place. He carried out his ablution in an excellent manner and then he said, "Whoever carries out ablution in this manner then comes to the mosque and prays two Rakʿahs without distracting his thoughts and then sits down [waiting for communal prayers], all his past sins are forgiven." He said the Prophet ﷺ said, "Don't get deluded."''

Ḥāfiẓ Ibn Ḥajar commented that this ḥadīth indicates that teaching with practice is preferable as it is more effective with the student. The Prophet ﷺ said, "Don't get deluded" meaning do not generalize the forgiveness of past sins to include all sins and worry less about sins relying on forgiveness through prayers. Prayers that erase sins are one that Allah accepts and no one knows that. In addition, prayers bring forgiveness only of minor sins, not major ones or trampled rights of others.

On one occasion the Prophet ﷺ led the prayers for the people while he was on the pulpit so that all of them could see him and could learn it by observing his actions.

❖ ḤADĪTH 22: Muslim and Bukhārī, the text is his reported[54] that Sahl ibn Saʿd as-Saʿīdī ؓ said, 'I saw the Messenger of Allah ﷺ standing on the pulpit, then he turned to the *qiblah* and said *Allahu Akbar*. People stood behind him while he recited [verses of the Qur'ān] and then bowed and people behind him bowed. He then raised his head, walked backward a little and then prostrated upon the ground. Thereafter he returned to the pulpit, then recited [verses of the Qur'ān] and bowed, he then raised his head and walked backward a little and prostrated upon the ground. When he completed his prayers he turned to the people and said, "O people! I did this only so that you may follow me and you may learn how I pray."

Imām Nawawī, in his commentary on *Ṣaḥīḥ* Muslim,[55] said, 'The Prophet explained to them that he went up the pulpit and prayed on it only to teach them so that all of them could see his actions, for had he stood on the ground only some of them who were close to him would have seen him.'

Ḥāfiẓ Ibn Ḥajar, in his commentary on *Ṣaḥīḥ* Bukhārī[56], said,

It is evident from what the Prophet ﷺ said, "O people! I did this so that you may follow me and learn how I pray" that the reason behind praying on the pulpit was to be seen by those who would not see him had he prayed on the floor.

The ḥadīth indicated that whoever does an unusual act he should explain the reason behind it to his associates and followers. It indicated the permissibility to teach the congregation the various acts of prayer by practicing it. It indicated the permissibility of slight movements during prayers. It indicated the permissibility of considerable movements in prayer if not done in sequence. It is preferable to use the pulpit since it enables the speaker to be seen and heard.

❖ ḤADĪTH **23:** Muslim, Abū Dāwūd and Ibn Mājah, the text is his reported[57] on the authority of Abū Saᶜīd al-Khudrī ﷺ that the Messenger of Allah ﷺ passed by a young man who was skinning a sheep. The Messenger of Allah ﷺ said to him, "Move aside so I may show you." Then the Messenger of Allah ﷺ inserted his hand between the skin and the flesh and pushed it until his armpit disappeared. He then said, "O young man! This is how you should skin." Then he ﷺ continued on his way and led the people in prayers without performing ablution.

Teaching the Sharīᶜah gradually

The Prophet ﷺ, in his teaching, adopted a gradual approach that prioritized taught topics according to their importance. He taught step by step to achieve ease of comprehension and better memorization.

❖ ḤADĪTH **24:** Ibn Mājah reported[58] on the authority of Jundab ibn ᶜAbdullah ﷺ who said, 'We were with the Prophet ﷺ while we were a group of youngsters close to the age of maturity. We learnt the tenets of faith before we learned the Qur'ān. Thereafter, we learnt the Qur'ān and that strengthened our faith.'

❖ ḤADĪTH **25:** Bukhārī and Muslim, the text is his reported[59] on the authority of Ibn ᶜAbbās (may Allah be pleased with both of them) that the Prophet ﷺ sent Muᶜādh to Yemen. The Prophet told him, "You will be travelling to a community of the People of the Book, invite them to declare that there no god but Allah and that I am the Messenger of Allah. If they accept that then tell them that Allah commanded them to give charity [*Zakāh*] to be taken from their wealthy and returned to their poor. If they obey that, never go after the best of their wealth and be conscious of the prayers of the oppressed for there is no barrier between it and Allah."

Among the many lessons of this ḥadīth are:

To start with the most important topic when calling or teaching; to demand the implementation of the requirements of the *Sharīᶜa* all at once would cause uneasiness.

Similarly, teaching all the different sciences at once to a student would cause the loss of all.

Imām Bukhārī has, in his *Ṣaḥīḥ*,[60] a subchapter titled 'Knowledge comes before sayings and actions'. Under this he wrote, 'It is said that 'a divinely scholar *Rabbānī* is he who teaches the people simple topics of knowledge before teaching them major ones." Ḥāfiẓ Ibn Ḥajar, in his comment on Imām Bukhārī, wrote, 'Little topics of knowledge mean clear and easy to understand issues while major ones are complex ones. Another explanation is that he teaches people details before general rules, secondary rules before principles, or introduction before objectives.'[61]

Ibn ᶜAbdul Barr quoted Yūnus ibn Yazīd who said Ibn Shihāb said to me, 'O Yūnus! Do not try to beat knowledge for it is like valleys that you will not be able to cross if you try to cross all at once. Learn knowledge along days and nights. Do not try to learn everything at once because whoever tries to learn everything at once loses it all. Learn one thing after another as days and nights pass.'[62]

❖ ḤADĪTH **26:** Imām Aḥmad reported[63] in his Collection on the authority Muḥammad Ibn Fuḍayl from ʿAṭā' – he is Ibn as-Sā'ib – on the authority of Abū ʿAbdur Raḥmān – he is as-Sulamī who said, 'The Companions of the Prophet ﷺ who used to teach us the Qur'ān told us that they used to learn from the Messenger of Allah ﷺ only ten verses. They would not move to the next ten verses until they had learnt what the first ten implied of knowledge and practice.'

❖ ḤADĪTH 27: aṭ-Ṭabarī reported in his Tafsīr[64], on the authority of al-Ḥusayn Ibn Wāqid who reported from al-Aʿmash from Shaqīq on the authority of Ibn Masʿūd ﷺ who said, 'When one of the men from us [i.e. the Companions] memorized ten verses, he would not go further until he learned their meanings and how to practice them.'

MODERATION AND STIMULATION

The Prophet ﷺ, when teaching his companions, was considerate of their time and readiness to receive his advice and learn from him. By being brief and reasonable he avoided bringing boredom to his companions.

❖ ḤADĪTH 28: Bukhārī reported this ḥadīth in his *Ṣaḥīḥ* in 'The Chapter of Knowledge' under a subchapter entitled 'the way the Prophet ﷺ used to handle reminding and teaching his companion so they would not become disinterested'. Muslim reported it in his *Ṣaḥīḥ* in the 'Chapter on Moderate Sermons', the wording is his.

On the authority of al-Aʿmash from Shaqīq Abū Wā'il who said, 'We were sitting at the door of ʿAbdullah ibn Masʿūd waiting for him when Yazīd ibn Muʿāwiyah an-Nakhaʿī came there. We asked Yazīd to tell him that we are here waiting for him to come out to us. He went inside and soon ʿAbdullah came out and said,

'I knew that you were waiting and what prevents me from coming out to you is that I hate to bore you. Indeed the Messenger of Allah ﷺ used to alternate his reminders during the day lest we get bored.'[65]

❖ ḤADĪTH 29: Bukhārī reported this ḥadīth also in his *Ṣaḥīḥ* in the 'Chapter of Knowledge' under a subchapter entitled 'Devoting certain days for the learners'. Muslim also reported it in his *Ṣaḥīḥ* in the 'Chapter on Moderate Sermons' and the wording is from both of them. On the authority of Manṣūr from Shaqīq Abū Wā'il said, "ʿAbdullah [ibn Masʿūd] used to give a reminder to the people every Thursday. A man said, 'O Abū ʿAbdur Raḥmān (this was a *Kunyah* for ʿAbdullah ibn Masʿūd), indeed we love your talk and we really look forward to it and we wish if you would preach to us every day.' He replied, 'The only thing preventing me from doing so is that I dislike boring you. I am alternating my preaching just as the Prophet ﷺ used to alternate with us, for the fear of making us bored.'

These two similar ḥadīths indicate many lessons: The Prophet ﷺ was considerate with his companions; he did not bombard them with preaching or information but alternated to make his words more interesting and effective. Boredom brings disinterest and distraction.

Ḥāfiẓ Ibn Ḥajar, in his Commentary, said: 'We learn from this ḥadīth the advisability of alternating between good deeds to avoid boredom. Continuity in practicing good deeds is desirable but in a one of two fashions: Practicing good deeds on daily basis but without any undue difficulty, or practicing them continuously but on alternate days. Resting a day will provide some respite. This may differ depending on circumstances and people. The criterion is the need for rest and stimulus.'

❖ ḤADĪTH **30:** Bukhārī reported this ḥadīth in his *Ṣaḥīḥ* in the 'Chapter of Knowledge' under a subchapter on 'How the Prophet ﷺ alternated his preaching lest they get disinterested'. Muslim also reported it in his *Ṣaḥīḥ* in the 'Chapter on Jihād'.[66]

Anas ibn Mālik ؓ said that the Prophet ﷺ said, "Bring ease not difficulty. Bring glad tidings not disaffection."

❖ ḤADĪTH **31:** Muslim reported a similar ḥadīth on the authority of Abū Mūsā al-Ashʿarī ؓ, who said, 'When the Messenger of Allah ﷺ sent one of his Companions on a task, he would say, "Bring glad tidings not disaffection. Bring ease not difficulty."

Imām Nawawī, in his Commentary on *Ṣaḥīḥ* Muslim[67], listed some of the lessons of this ḥadīth:

The ḥadīth commands us to give glad tidings of Allah's grace, great rewards, plentiful gifts and all-encompassing mercy.

The ḥadīth forbids us from spreading disaffection by only citing frightening topics and fearsome punishments without combining it with glad tidings as well.

The ḥadīth directs us to bring new Muslims closer to Islam by being flexible and less stringent with them. This rule applies also to adolescents and to those who recently renounced their sins. All should be dealt with kindness and gradually steered to perform the various acts of obedience.

The duties of Islam were assigned gradually. It will be easier to fulfill and eventually to build on, if it were made easy for newcomers or those contemplating to join. If it were made difficult, newcomers may find it too daunting to practice and if they practice it they may not maintain it or enjoy it.

Ḥāfiẓ Ibn Ḥajar, in his Commentary on Bukhārī, said, 'Disseminating knowledge must be done gradually, because if a matter was introduced smoothly, it will be liked by those tackling it and they will gladly accept it and, most likely, will go for more, something they may not do if it was difficult at its beginning.'[68]

Individual differences among students

The Prophet ﷺ was very much aware of the individual differences among the learners and enquirers and addressed each according to his intellectual level and in a way that was appropriate to their status. He was keen to maintain the beginners stimulated and, therefore, did not teach them what he used to teach senior students. He used to answer the question of each person according to what was important to that person and was appropriate for his conditions.

❖ ḤADĪTH 32: Bukhārī reported this ḥadīth in his *Ṣaḥīḥ* in the 'Chapter of Knowledge' under a subchapter on 'Excluding some people from certain teaching lest they do not understand it'. Muslim also reported it in his *Ṣaḥīḥ* in the 'Chapter of Faith' and the wording is from both of them. Anas ibn Mālik ﷺ said, 'The Prophet of Allah ﷺ was on his camel and Muʿādh ibn Jabal ﷺ was riding directly behind him. The Prophet said, "O Muʿādh!" 'Yes, Messenger of Allah I am at your disposal', Muʿādh responded. The Prophet repeated, "O Muʿādh!" And Muʿādh replied, 'Messenger of Allah I am at your disposal.' The Prophet again said, "O Muʿādh!" And Muʿādh replied, 'Messenger of Allah I am at your disposal.'

The Prophet said, "Every slave who testifies, with complete sincerity, that there is no god but Allah and that Muḥammad is his servant and messenger, Allah shall forbid Hell's fire from touching him" Muʿādh said, 'O Messenger of Allah, should I not inform the people about this so to bring them glad tidings?' He replied, "No. Because then they will become lax." Muʿādh disclosed this before his death lest he [conceal knowledge and] commit a sin.

The ḥadīth indicates the following guidance:

The Prophet ﷺ asked Muʿādh ﷺ not to tell people about this mercy of Allah because they will have a superficial understanding of it and will think that to escape hellfire it is enough to declare the oneness of God and the prophecy of the Prophet. They will not pay attention that a declaration of faith carries duties that include obeying Allah and his messenger in life and laws.

Imām al-Badr al-ʿAynī, in his commentary on *Ṣaḥīḥ* Bukhārī[69], said: The ḥadīth indicates the advisability of providing intricate knowledge only to those who are accurate and thoughtful in their understanding. It should not be imparted to students who would not understand it or to those who may falsely rely on it due to their lack of understanding.

Ḥāfiẓ ibn Rajab, in his commentary on *Ṣaḥīḥ* Bukhārī[70], said, 'The scholars concluded from the refusal of the Prophet that it is advisable not to disseminate among the ignorant ḥadīths containing licenses lest they become lax, as they may miss its true significance. Muʿādh, for example, heard this but it only prompted him to increase his endeavour of good deeds and observance of Allah. One would fear that others who lack his perspective may become lax after relying on the literal meaning of this ḥadīth.'

This approach of not teaching everything to anyone was adapted by the companions and scholars. Imām Bukhārī reported, under the heading mentioned above, on the authority of 'Alī, 'Tell people what they can understand; would you like it that Allah and his messenger be rejected?' Adam ibn Abī Iyas, in his narration, added, 'and leave out what may baffle them.'

That 'Allah and his messenger might be rejected' means that when a person hears something he does not understand and or conceive to be possible, he may, ignorantly, reject it right away. If something like this is reported about the Prophet, he will hasten to reject it and consequently rejecting the word of Allah.

Ḥāfiẓ Ibn Ḥajar, in his commentary on Bukhārī[71], said, 'This ḥadīth indicates that paradoxical issues should not be reviewed with laypeople. This is confirmed by the opinion of Ibn Masʿūd[72] who said, 'When you tell a group something beyond their understanding, it is inevitable that it become a dilemma for some of them.'

This was the opinion of other scholars. Imām Aḥmad disliked narration of ḥadīths apparently encouraging revolt; likewise Imām Mālik disliked narration of ḥadīths that pertains to the attributes of Allah that may give the impression He is similar to human beings. Imām Abū Yūsuf disliked narration of odd ḥadīths. Even this was the view of earlier generations like Abū Hurayrah and Ḥudhayfah. The criterion governing this is the judgment that a ḥadīth could be construed, if understood superficially, to encourage deviation, which is not what it meant. If this was the case, then it is required to withhold it from those who misunderstand it and apply it superficially.'

This is a key principle of teaching; the teacher carefully consider the level of his students' intelligence and understanding and teach them what is appropriate for their intellect while deferring what is not. Imām Al-Ghazālī said in the *Iḥyā'*[73], 'Among the responsibilities of the teacher is to observe in his teaching the extent of the student's understanding; he should not teach him something beyond his intellect since that will turn away from studying or will leave him baffled or confused. In the first, he will be following the method the leader of humanity, Muḥammad ﷺ who used to take this into consideration in his teaching, talks and sermons.

But the teacher should disseminate knowledge to the student if he knew he is capable of comprehending it on his own. It is not advisable for a scholar to impart all his knowledge to everyone. This applies even if the student understands what he is being taught but would not benefit from it and hence it is more applicable if he cannot understand it! A person rightly said, 'Measure for each according to his intellect and weigh for him according to his understanding. This way he will not blame you and will indeed benefit from you. Otherwise he may denounce you due to disparity in standards.'

When Allah said, 'Do not give your wealth to foolish people.' He drew our attention that it is more important to withhold knowledge from those who will be spoiled and harmed by it. The injustice of giving those who are undeserved is not less than depriving those who deserve.'

'A beginner student should be taught what is clear and appropriate to his intellect without telling him that, beyond this, there are more intricate issues that were withheld from him. This may cause the student to lose interest in learning the essentials and leave him confused. He may even think his teacher is disfavouring him since everyone believes that he himself is capable of understanding all intricate knowledge.

Further, intricate issues should not be discussed with laypeople. Rather, they should be taught how to perform their acts of worship and the importance of honesty in the businesses they conduct. He should fill their hearts with desire for paradise and fear of hell just as the Qur'ān had done so. He should not raise doubtful issues as such doubts may embellish their thoughts and become too persistent to remove and ultimately causing dejection and doom.'

Imām Abū ʿAmr ibn as-Ṣalāh, in his commentary on *Ṣaḥīḥ* Muslim[74], said, 'Why would Muʿādh tell this at the time of his death though the Prophet prohibited him from telling people? My explanation is that the Prophet prohibited him from giving this glad tiding publicly lest it is heard by those who lack understanding and experience and who might be lured by their misunderstanding to become lax. Even though, the Prophet told this privately to those who enjoyed insight and comprehension and whom he trusted they would not fall prey to ignorance and complacency. This is why he told Muʿādh and Muʿādh for the fear of hiding knowledge from those who deserve it, followed the example of the Prophet and he only informed people whom he felt were worthy of it. And Allah knows best.'

❖ ḤADĪTH 33: Imām Aḥmad reported[75] in his *Musnad* on the authority of ʿAbdullah ibn ʿAmr ibn al-ʿĀṣ (may Allah be pleased with both of them), who said, 'We were with the Prophet ﷺ when a young man came and asked, 'O Messenger of Allah! Can I kiss [my wife] whilst I am fasting?' "No" the Prophet answered. Thereafter an old man came and asked, 'Can I kiss [my wife] while I am fasting?' "Yes" the Prophet responded. As we were exchanging looks the Messenger of Allah ﷺ said, "I know why you are exchanging looks; indeed the old man can control himself."'

This ḥadīth reinforces and illustrates the point of changing the answer based on the enquirer. Since the old man can control himself, there is no fear that a kiss will lead him to intercourse and void his fast. As for the young man, kissing may lead him to intercourse or ejaculation and thus nullify his fast.

❖ ḤADĪTH 34: Bukhārī and Muslim reported[76] on the authority of ʿAbdullah ibn ʿAmr ibn al-ʿĀṣ who said, 'A man came to the Prophet ﷺ seeking his permission to participate in *Jihād*. The Prophet asked him, "Are your parents alive?" 'Yes' the man replied. The Prophet said, "With them is your *Jihād*."'

The implication here is to do your best to be kind and generous to your parents. This, for you, is equal to *Jihād* and fighting the enemy.

❖ ḤADĪTH **35:** Muslim reported[77] on the authority of ʿAbdullah ibn ʿAmr ibn al-ʿĀṣ who said, 'A man came to the Prophet of Allah ﷺ and said, 'I would like to give you my pledge of allegiance for emigration and *Jihād* seeking reward from Allah.' The Prophet asked, "Are any of your parents alive?" 'Yes. Indeed both of them' he replied. The Prophet said, "And you seek reward from Allah?" 'Yes' the man said. The Prophet responded, "Return to your parents and perfect your companionship of them."'

The Prophet ﷺ gave this reply despite his known keenness to promote participation in *Jihād* and *Hijrah*, but he took into consideration the specifics of this young man and reasoned that looking after his parents was more important and more virtuous for him.

The variation of the Prophet's replies according to differences of conditions, circumstances and abilities of those who asked him is a well established principle that has numerous examples in the books of the *Sunnah*. Among these replies are his different advices to those who sought it, whereby he gave a different advice to each due to differences in their individual circumstances.

❖ ḤADĪTH **36:** Tirmidhī and Imām Aḥmad and the wording is his reported[78] on the authority of Abū Dharr ؓ who said, 'I said, 'O Messenger of Allah! Give me some advice.' The Prophet replied, "Fear Allah wherever you may be and follow up a bad deed with a good one and it will wipe it out. Deal with people in a noble manner."'

V ḤADĪTH **37:** Bukhārī and Tirmidhī reported[79] and the wording is from both of them, on the authority of Abū Hurayrah ؓ, who said, 'that a man said to the Prophet ﷺ, 'Give me some advice; a brief one so I can remember it.' The Prophet said, "Don't get angry." The person repeated his request several times and each time the Prophet said to him, "Don't get angry."'

Imām al-Khaṭṭabī, in his commentary on Bukhārī, said[80] that "Don't get angry" means 'Do not expose yourself to reasons and conditions that will provoke your anger. Anger is an entrenched human trait that is impossible to remove. Another angle to this ḥadīth is that you should not do what your anger dictates and pushes you to do or to say.'

❖ ḤADĪTH 38: Bukhārī and Muslim and the text is his reported[81] on the authority of Abū Hurayrah ﷺ 'that a desert arab came to the Messenger of Allah ﷺ and said, 'O Messenger of Allah! Show me a deed which if I carried out, I will enter paradise.' The Prophet replied, "Worship Allah without associating anything with Him, establish the mandatory prayers, give the prescribed *Zakāh* and fast the month of Ramaḍān." The desert arab responded, 'By Allah in whose hand is my life, I will never do more or less than this.' When the desert arab went away, the Prophet ﷺ said, "Whoever likes to see a person from Paradise, should look at him."'

I would like to point out that such words of glad tidings "a person from Paradise" are sometimes said about some pious people. However, we should refrain from saying it as it implies that such a person is definitely among the people of Paradise, but this is known only by Allah and His Messenger through divine revelation.

❖ ḤADĪTH 39: Ibn Mājah and Tirmidhī and the text is his reported[82] on the authority of ʿAbdullah ibn Busr 'that A man said, 'O Messenger of Allah! The rules of Islam became too many for me. So inform me of something that I could hold on to.' The Prophet said, "Let your tongue be always moist with the remembrance of Allah."'

❖ ḤADĪTH 40: Muslim, Tirmidhī and Ibn Mājah reported[83]

on the authority of Sufyān ibn ʿAbdullah ath-Thaqafī who said, 'I said, 'O Messenger of Allah! Tell me some words about Islam so I need not ask anyone after you.' The Prophet said, "Say, 'I believe in Allah and then remain steadfast.'"' This is the wording of Muslim. The narration of Tirmidhī and Ibn Mājah[84] is, 'I said, 'O Messenger of Allah! Tell me something to hold on to.' The Prophet said, "Say, 'My Lord is Allah. And then remain steadfast.'" I asked, 'O Messenger of Allah! What do you fear most for me?' The Prophet held his own tongue and said, "This."'

❖ ḤADĪTH **41:** Tirmidhī reported[85] on the authority of ʿUqbah ibn ʿĀmir ﷺ who said, 'I said, 'O Messenger of Allah! What is salvation?' He said, "Control your tongue, remain in your house and shed tears over your own faults."' There are other traditions that fall under this category and demonstrate that the succinct advices of the Prophet varied to take into consideration the circumstances and needs of those who sought it. For the same reason, the Prophet varied his replies when asked about most virtuous deeds or most liked by Allah. He answered each with what he felt was the best for him in general or at that particular moment based on his needs and situation.

❖ ḤADĪTH **42:** Bukhārī and Muslim and the text is his reported[86] on the authority of ʿAbdullah ibn ʿAmr (may Allah, the Exalted be pleased with both of them) that a man asked the Messenger of Allah ﷺ, 'Which part of Islam is the best?' "That you feed [people] food and greet your acquaintances as well as strangers." Replied the Prophet.'

❖ ḤADĪTH **43:** Muslim reported[87] on the authority of Abdullah ibn ʿAmr (may Allah, the Exalted be pleased with both of them) that a man asked the Messenger of Allah ﷺ, 'Which Muslim is the best?' "He whom Muslims are safe from his tongue and his hand." The Prophet replied.

❖ ḤADĪTH 44: Muslim and Bukhārī (the text is his) reported[88] on the authority of Abū Hurayra ﷺ who said, 'The Prophet ﷺ was asked, 'Which deed is the most virtuous?' He replied, "Belief in Allah and His messenger." He was asked, 'Then what?' He replied, "Jihād in the cause of Allah." He was asked, 'Then what?' He replied, "An accepted Hajj."

❖ ḤADĪTH 45: Bukhārī and Muslim (the text is his) reported[89] on the authority of ʿAbdullah ibn Masʿūd ﷺ who said, 'I asked the Messenger of Allah ﷺ 'Which deed is the most virtuous?' (in another narration, 'Which deed is the most liked by Allah?') "Praying on time," he replied. He said, I asked, 'Then which?' "Kindness to parents," he replied and he said, I asked, 'Then which?' He replied, "Jihād in the cause of Allah." I refrained from asking him more lest I bother him.'

Imām Nawawī, in his commentary on *Ṣaḥīḥ* Muslim[90], said that Ibn Masʿūd ﷺ did not continue asking about the rest of deeds and its order in virtue out of consideration for the Prophet ﷺ. This ḥadīth teaches that the student must be careful with the teacher and considerate and thoughtful of his needs.

❖ ḤADĪTH 46: Abū Yaʿlā reported[91] on the authority of a man from the tribe of 'Khathʿam who said, 'I came to the Prophet ﷺ whilst he was with a group of his companions. I said to him, 'Are you the one who claims that you are the messenger of Allah?' He replied, "Yes." I asked, 'O Messenger of Allah! Which deed is most liked by Allah?' He replied, "Belief in Allah." He said, I asked, 'O Messenger of Allah! Then which?' He replied, "Then taking good care of your kin." He said, I asked, "O Messenger of Allah! Then which?' He replied, "Then enjoining good and forbidding evil."

He said, I asked, 'O Messenger of Allah! Which deed is most disliked by Allah?' He replied, "Associating partners with Allah." He said, I asked, 'O Messenger of Allah! Then which?' He replied, "Then severing ties of kinship." He said, I asked, 'O Messenger of Allah! Then which?' He replied, "Commanding evil and prohibiting good."'

The previous ḥadīth directs the teacher, or the Muftī, to be tolerant with the one he gives Fatwā to or teaches and to bear the vast amounts of his questions and reports.

There are other similar ḥadīths where the replies of the Prophet ﷺ varied with regard to the best or most preferred deeds and the variation reflects the individual differences amongst the enquirers, whether individuals or groups, or the particular timings of their questions. The Prophet ﷺ guided each to what they needed most or to Islamic tenets that they have not learned and its knowledge had not reached them, or to what befits their interests or status.

Or he could have informed the enquirer of the most preferred deed at that particular time. For the nascent Islam, Jihād was the most virtuous deed because it enabled the performance of other deeds and fulfilment of obligations. Many traditions point that prayers are more virtuous than Zakat, although the latter becomes more virtuous when it alleviates the immediate needs of the deprived.

Some of the variance in answers could be attributed to the wording of the questions and to the Prophet ﷺ observing that virtue could not be confined to one attribute and one aspect. Rather, virtue has many manifestations and rankings and varying replies might reflect the Prophet's consideration of individual differences between various facets of virtue and ways to goodness.[92]

The Prophet ﷺ indeed was the considerate teacher and the

insightful guide. He enlightens each person with what he appropriately needs. May Allah, the Exalted send prayers, bless and shower peace upon him and his family.

DIALOGUE & QUESTIONS

Dialogue and questions are the Prophet's most prominent methods of teaching since that draws the attention of the listeners, arouse their curiosity to know the answer and prompt them to reflect on the answer. If they were unable to provide an answer, the answer of the Prophet will be well understood and entrenched in their minds.

❖ ḤADĪTH 47: Bukhārī and Muslim (the text is his) reported[93] on the authority of Abū Hurayra ﷺ who said, 'The Messenger of Allah ﷺ said, "If there was a river by the door of one of you and he was to bath therein five times daily, will any dirt remain on him?" They replied, 'No dirt will remain on him.' The Prophet said, "This resembles the five daily prayers; Allah wipes off sins with them."'

In this ḥadīth, we see, beside dialogue, other educational methods such as bringing an abstract concept into a tangible understanding to it make very clear and understandable to the student. In this example, the Prophet ﷺ compared the cleansing of tangible dirt on the body and clothes with ample clean water to the five daily prayers and how it cleanses the sins and faults of the worshipper.

❖ ḤADĪTH 48: Imām Aḥmad reported[94] in his *Musnad* on the

authority of ʿAbdullah ibn ʿAmr ibn al-ʿĀṣ (may Allah be pleased with both of them), who said, 'I heard the Messenger of Allah saying, "Do you know who the Muslim is?" The companions replied, 'Allah and his messenger know best.' He said, "A Muslim is he from whose tongue and hands other Muslims are safe." He asked, "Do you know who the believer is?" The companions said, 'Allah and his messenger know best.' He said, "He is whom the Believers trusted with their lives and their wealth. And an emigrant (*Muhajir*) is he who left evil and abstained from it."'

That the Prophet ﷺ used here the words "Muslims" and "Believers" not to allow disagreeable behaviour with others. He used it to match the words "the Muslim" and "the Believer." Inflicting harm or betraying trust is forbidden in Islam whether with Muslims or non-Muslims except in war. I believe that harming or cheating non-Muslims is more forbidden as the Prophet ﷺ warned that he will be the plaintiff in such a case as reported in the authentic ḥadīth by Abū Dāwūd in his *Sunan*: "Let it be known that whoever was unfair to a peaceful non-Muslim, disparaged him, or burdened him above capacity, or took something from him against his will, I shall be his opponent on the day of resurrection."

❖ ḤADĪTH **49:** Muslim reported[95] on the authority of Abū Hurayra ﷺ who said, 'The Messenger of Allah ﷺ said, "Do you know who the bankrupt one is?" They [the companions] replied, 'The bankrupt one amongst us is he who has neither any dirham nor any possessions.' He said, "The bankrupt one in my Ummah is he who comes on the Day of Resurrection with his prayers, fasting and Zakat, but he comes after he had swore at this person, slandered this person, devoured the wealth of this person, shed the blood of this person and beaten this person. This person will be given from his good deeds and this person will be given from his good deeds. If all his good deeds are finished before he has paid them back, their evil deeds will be taken from them and cast onto him. He will then be cast into the hellfire."'

Here, the Prophet ﷺ started by asking a question and then detailed the answer to his question. This was to draw their attention that the real bankruptcy is the bankruptcy on the Day of Resurrection.

Among the most famous examples of teaching through dialogue is the ḥadīth of Jibrīl ﷺ teaching the tenets of faith that ʿUmar ibn al-Khaṭṭāb ﷺ and other than him from the companions narrated. The most important tenets of faith were shown to the companions in the form of a dialogue between the Messenger ﷺ and Jibrīl ﷺ that covered the principles of their religion.

❖ ḤADĪTH 50: Muslim and others reported[96] on the authority of ʿUmar ibn al-Khaṭṭāb ﷺ who said, 'One day, while we were in the company of the Messenger of Allah ﷺ, a man appeared before us wearing a very white clothing and having pitch black hair. The effects of travelling were not noticeable on him and none of us knew him. He came forward till he sat in front of the Prophet ﷺ he placed his knees against the Prophet's knees and he placed his hands on his own thighs.

The man then said, 'O Muḥammad! Tell me about Islam.' So the Messenger of Allah ﷺ said, "Islam is to testify that there is no god but Allah and that Muḥammad is the Messenger of Allah, to establish prayer, to give alms *Zakāt*, to fast the month of Ramaḍān and to make pilgrimage to the House if you have the means to do so."

The man said, 'You have spoken the truth.' ʿUmar ﷺ said, 'We wondered at him, asking the Prophet and then affirming the answer.'

The man then said, 'Tell me about faith *īmān*.' The Prophet replied, "To believe in Allah, His angels, His books, His messengers, the last day and to believe in pre-destiny, its good and its bad thereof." The man said, 'You have spoken the truth.'

Then the man said, 'Tell me about perfection *Iḥsān*.' The Prophet said, "To worship Allah as though you are seeing Him, for if you cannot see Him, He sees you."

Then the man said, 'Tell me about the Hour.' The Prophet replied, "The one being asked does not know more than the one asking." The man said, 'Tell me about its signs.' The Prophet said, "The slave-girl will give birth to her master. You will see shepherds who are barefooted, naked and paupers competing with each other in building lofty buildings."

ʿUmar ﷺ said, 'Then the man left. I waited for a considerable time before the Prophet ﷺ said to me, "O ʿUmar! Do you know who the enquirer was?" I said, 'Allah and His messenger know best.' He said, "That was Jibrīl; he came to teach you all your religion."

This ḥadīth has many points to ponder and many lessons to be learnt:

The companions were surprised about the man saying to the Prophet ﷺ, 'You have spoken the truth' since, usually, a person asks a question because he doesn't know the answer. Even more surprising was this because affirmation implies knowing the answer, but most of these answers could be only known to, or from, the Prophet ﷺ. However, this man was not known to have ever met the Prophet ﷺ let alone learning from him. Some narrations depict this better:

'We never saw a man like him; it was as if he was teaching the Messenger o Allah ﷺ, saying to him, 'You have spoken the truth, you have spoken the truth.'

Imām Nawawī, in his commentaries on *Ṣaḥīḥ* Muslim[97] and *Ṣaḥīḥ* Bukhārī, said[98], 'Imagine if one of us commenced an act of worship while witnessing his Lord ﷻ; he would not leave out anything he could do with regards to humility, submission, nice attire, focusing his outward and inner self to ensure that his act is perfect in the best way. The Prophet ﷺ said, "that you should worship Allah in all situations as you would do if you are indeed seeing Him." The perfection if you are seeing Him is prompted by your knowledge that He sees what you are doing and, hence, you will not overlook anything as Allah is watching you. Remember that this is true and applicable even if you do not really see Allah, so you should act accordingly.

The purpose of these words is to urge sincerity in worship and observance of his Lord ﷻ in attaining complete humility and submission, etc... The Sufis recommend accompanying the pious to steer you away from the slightest shortcoming out of respect and diffidence for them. How about if you are aware that Allah, the Exalted knows what you do whether in private or in public?

The ḥadīth focuses our mind that we will observe these manners, if we see Allah and He sees us, because *he sees us* and not because we see Him. As He sees us all the time, we should worship Him with perfection even if we do not see Him. The ḥadīth tells us that even though we don't see Allah, we should continue worshipping Him perfectly, as He definitely sees us.'

Imām Nawawī concluded by saying, 'This part of the ḥadīth is an important principle of Islam and an important rule for Muslims. It is the central creed of sincere believers, the ultimate goal of the strivers, the treasure of those in the know and the passion of the righteous. These words are among the succinct, but meaningful, statements that Allah endowed the Prophet ﷺ with.'

When asked about the Hour, the Prophet ﷺ did not say, 'I do not know about it more than you do.' He said, "The one being asked does not know more than the one asking" in order to point out that everyone who is being asked or asking about the timing of the Hour does not know it. Imām Nawawī, in his commentary on Muslim[99] said, 'We can deduce from this that when a scholar or a Muftī and other them are asked about what they do not know, they should say, 'I do not know.' This will not diminish his status but, to the contrary, points to his dedication, his piety and wealth of his knowledge.'

The Prophet ﷺ listed among the signs of the Hour "The slave-girl will give birth to her master." This is a metaphorical expression pointing out that maltreatment of parents will be widespread among children to the extent that a child will treat his own parents as a master may treat his slave with abuse, beating and servitude.

The purpose of these signs is to foresee a change in living conditions when rural people will forcibly usurp power, increase their wealth and focus their efforts on competing with others over construction of magnificent buildings. Other authentic ḥadīths spoke about:

"The Hour will only come when the happiest people on earth are wicked ones, the children of wicked ones."

And, "When power is in hands that do not deserve it; then expect the Hour."

Among the educational benefits of this ḥadīth is that if a person joined a scholar in his class and felt a need to ask a question that others are hesitant to ask, he should ask the question to benefit all.[100]

The ḥadīth directs the scholar to be approachable and understanding with the enquirer to put him at complete ease with his questions. Likewise, the questioner should also be courteous when posing his questions as pointed out by Imām Nawawī in his commentary of Muslim.

It is permissible to ask a question to the scholar, which one already knows its answer so that others present may also learn it.

The Prophet ﷺ termed Jibrīl ﷺ as a teacher when he said, "That was Jibrīl; he came to teach you all your religion." This indicates that a good question is part of the learning and teaching process. Jibrīl ﷺ only posed the questions and the Prophet ﷺ referred to him as a teacher. A common saying among scholars is that 'a good question is half the learning process.'

Judge ʿĪyāḍ said that, 'the ḥadīth of Jibrīl covered the explanation of all outward and inner acts of worship. It commenced with essentials of faith, physical acts, purity of intentions, avoiding the consequence of evil deeds. All the aspects of the *Sharīʿa* could be derived from this ḥadīth; whether it was an injunction, a commendable or desired deed, a prohibition, or an undesirable act. All are within its three divisions, namely: belief, practice and perfection.'[101]

Teaching through dialogue and rational comparison

Rational comparison laid out through questions and answers was among the methods the Prophet ﷺ used in his teaching especially to unveil the ugliness of evil to those who admired it or to reinforce truth in the heart of those who considered it incredible or implausible. I will cite one ḥadīth of each type:

❖ ḤADĪTH **51:** Ṭabarānī and Aḥmad, the text is his, reported[102] on the authority of Abū Umāmah al-Bāhilī ﷺ, 'that a young man came to the Prophet ﷺ and said, 'O Messenger of Allah! Permit me to commit fornication.' Those present turned to him, rebuked him and they told him to 'stop stop!'

He ﷺ said, "Come to me." So he went and sat down near the Prophet. He ﷺ said to him, "Would you like it to happen to your mother?" 'By God, No! O Messenger of Allah, may Allah make me your ransom,' the young man replied. He ﷺ said, "And people also loath it for their mothers."

He ﷺ said, "Would you like it to happen to your daughter?" 'By God, No! O Messenger of Allah, may Allah make me your ransom,' the young man replied. He ﷺ said, "And people also loath it for their daughters."

He ﷺ said, "Would you like it to happen to your sister?" 'By God, No! O Messenger of Allah, may Allah make me your ransom,' the young man replied. He ﷺ said, "And people also loath it for their sisters."

He ﷺ said, "Would you like it to happen to your paternal aunt?" 'By God, No! O Messenger of Allah, may Allah make me your ransom,' the young man replied. He ﷺ said, "And people also loath it for their paternal aunts."

He ﷺ said, "Would you like it to happen to your maternal aunt?" 'By God, No! O Messenger of Allah, may Allah make me your ransom,' the young man replied. He ﷺ said, "And people also loath it for their maternal aunts."

He said, 'then the Messenger of Allah ﷺ placed his hand on [the chest of] the young man and prayed, "O Allah! Forgive his sin, purify his heart and reinforce his chastity."

The narrator said, 'The young man never looked at anything thereafter.'

We should reflect at how the Prophet ﷺ, through dialogue, inner reflection and rational comparison, completely uprooted the urge of this young man towards fornication. The Prophet ﷺ achieved this without citing the Qur'ānic verses that prohibit fornication and forewarn of punishment for fornicators whether men or women. The Prophet ﷺ resorted to this method because it was, at that moment, the most effective in removing this vice from the heart of the young man based on his perception and understanding.

This is a guidance for callers to Allah to resort to logic at certain times or with certain people when the situation merits so, as was the case of this young man whose heart the Prophet ﷺ cleansed of fornication through calm use of logical comparison. As for the second type:

❖ **ḤADĪTH 52:** Bukhārī (the text is his) and Muslim reported[103] on the authority of Abū Saʿīd al-Khudrī who said, 'The Messenger of Allah ﷺ went out to the prayer field either on 'īd al-Fiṭr or 'īd al-Aḍḥā. He then said, "O group of women! Donate to charity for indeed I have been shown you to be too many among those in hell-fire." They asked, 'Why is that, O Messenger of Allah?' He ﷺ said, "You curse a lot and you are unthankful to your husbands. I have not seen like you someone of less logic and religiosity causing a resolute man to lose his mind." They asked, 'O Messenger of Allah! What is less about our logic and religiosity?' He replied, "Is not the testimony of a woman equal to half the testimony of a man?" They replied, 'Indeed.' the Prophet said, "That is the deficiency of her logic. Is it not when a woman is menstruating that she neither prays nor fasts?" They replied, 'Indeed.' The Prophet said, "That is the deficiency of her religion."

Asking the Companions to Stimulate Their Intelligence and Knowledge

At times the Prophet ﷺ would ask his companions about something that he knew well. He just asked them to stimulate their insight, stir up their intelligence and convey knowledge to them in the form of a puzzle to test how knowledgeable they were.

ḥadīth 53: Bukhārī and Muslim reported[104] on the authority of ʿAbdullah ibn ʿUmar (may Allah be pleased with both of them) who said, 'We were sitting in the company of the Prophet ﷺ when he was brought an edible palm core. While eating it, he said, "Indeed amongst the trees there is an evergreen tree and its goodness and benefits are like that of the Muslim. Its leaves do not fall nor do they scatter around. It produces its fruit at its appropriate time by its Lord's permission and it is similar to the Muslim. Tell me which tree it is?"

ᶜAbdullah ﷺ said, 'People started naming the trees of the desert; this tree and that tree. I felt that it was the palm tree and I wanted to say so but as a young man in the presence of elders I was hesitant to talk; I looked around the ten people there and I was the youngest. I saw Abū Bakr and ᶜUmar silent so I kept silent. So when neither of them spoke, they said, 'Messenger of Allah! Tell us what it is?' The Messenger of Allah ﷺ said, "It is the palm tree."

When we left I told ᶜUmar my father, 'O father, by Allah I thought it was the palm tree!' He asked, 'What prevented you from saying that?' I said, 'I didn't see you talk. I didn't see you or Abū Bakr talking and I am a young man. So I felt shy and disliked saying something so I remained silent.' ᶜUmar responded, 'I wish that you would have said it that would have been dearer to me than having such and such."

Lessons of the ḥadīth:

There are many similarities between the date palm and the believer. It is one of the noblest of trees and of the highest in standing when one considers its abundant gifts, shade at all time, tasty fruits that could be available all year round starting when it appears till its harvest and beyond. When the date palm dies it remains useful; its wood, leaves and branches are used for stumps, firewood, staffs, ropes, utensils, etc… Beside that, date-pits are used as fodder for camels.

Those who live in the Arabian Peninsula know very well and benefit so much from the many qualities of the date palm; the beautiful sight of its growth and leaves, its beautiful shape and fruit, its elegant and lofty height, its evergreen leaves, the strength of its trunk that withstands winds and storms and its generous shade and shelter. Allah showered praise on it in several verses of the Qur'ān.

Likewise the Muslim or the believer is the source of goodness and benefit that is readily available to himself and to others at all times even after his death. His deeds are good, his words are beautiful and his worship of Allah is abundant be it fasting, prayers, recitation of the Qur'ān, remembrance of Allah, reminding others of Allah, giving in charity, enjoining goodness and denouncing evil. He socialises with people and overlooks their faults. He is at ease with people and so they are with him. He benefits and does not harm others and his outward appearance is nice as well as his inner self and his good manners are offered readily to people. He gives and does not hold back, he is unselfish and not greedy. He remains at all times towering high above callousness. Hardships and ordeals only make him more firm and resolute to defend the truth, aspiring to spread goodness and benefit others and he is wary of petty talk.

His deeds are ascending to his Lord with acceptance and pleasure. He will always benefit you if you sit with him, if you partner him, if you accompany him and if you consult him. His benefits are boundless and what you may learn from him is that which is nourishing for souls and hearts. His religion is his protection, never devoid of piety and always generating good deeds whether he is rich or poor, or healthy or sick. His works continue even after his death, for he had prepared in his life for the later life and prepared today for tomorrow. He enjoys all of this whether dead or alive for the revolving point of all his deeds is his belief in Allah and benefitting the servants of Allah. Glory be to Allah, how great the believer is!

Imām Bukhārī reported this ḥadīth eleven times under different headings in his *Ṣaḥīḥ*. I would like to cite it all since it constitutes a brief commentary on the ḥadīth. In the Chapter of Knowledge he cited it under 'A narrator saying, 'He said to us, he told us and he informed us', 'The Imām posing a question to his companions to probe their knowledge', 'Understanding in learning' and 'Shyness in learning'. In the Chapter of Transactions he cited it under 'Selling a palm core and eating it.' In the Chapter of Tafsīr he cited it under 'The explication of Sūra Ibrāhīm.' In the Chapter of Food he cited it under 'Eating palm cores' and 'The blessing of the date palm'. In the Chapter of Manners he cited it twice under 'What one should not be shy about when seeking to increase his religious knowledge' and 'Honouring the elders and giving them privilege of talking and asking first'. In addition to Imām Muslim who cited it five times, other scholars of ḥadīth, such as Imām Aḥmad, reported this ḥadīth. I've gathered all these narrations and elaborated on the ḥadīth in a public lecture that I delivered in Rabat, Morocco in Ramadan 1387 at the invitation of King Hasan II.

I would like to summarise what the comments of the great scholar and literary master Shaikh Abū-l-ḥasan al-ḥasanī an-Nadawī, whom I am honoured to be his friend, in his introduction to the book of our great Shaikh and scholar of ḥadīth Maulana Muḥammad Zakariyyā al-Kāndahlawī 'The Chapters and Biographies of Bukhārī':

'It is common knowledge among scholars that the *fiqh* of Imām Bukhārī is manifested in the biographies of his *Ṣaḥīḥ*. Bukhārī enjoyed a wide perspective, great intellect, sharp intelligence and a deep understanding of the crux of the ḥadīth coupled with a keen sense of extracting all what could be learned from it. Thus, he would cite a single ḥadīth in different chapters under many headings, categories and subjects. He is like a bee that is earnest to draw from the flower all the nectar to the last drop and convert it to pure honey that will bring health to people.

Imām Bukhārī was enamoured with the authentic ḥadīth. As true lovers would look at their love and see beauty and perfection that never ends and always fresh and surprising, Imām Bukhārī never ceases to find topics and derive lessons deep amongst the meaning of the ḥadīth, all to present it to his readers to the extent that he will cite a single ḥadīth twenty different times. He cited the ḥadīth of Barīra on the authority of ʿĀ'isha more than twenty two times and derived many rules and benefits from it. He cited the ḥadīth of Jābir and the Prophet ﷺ buying his camel more than twenty times. He cited eleven times the ḥadīth of ʿĀ'isha that the Prophet ﷺ bought food, on credit, from a Jew and gave him his shield as a guarantee. He cited eleven times the ḥadīth of Ibn ʿUmar on the date palm and detailed its benefits.

The secret of this is that Imām Bukhārī did not limit himself to just examining the ḥadīth to derive rules of fiqh like what other fiqh and ḥadīth scholars did. Rather he would thoroughly examine the ḥadīth and derive practical and scientific lessons that do not fall under the traditional categories of fiqh. May Allah bless his sole.'

Now, I will list major educational benefits that could be learned from this noble ḥadīth:

Starting with the advisability that the scholar puts a question to his companions to probe their understanding and to encourage them to reflect and to be thorough. He would then explain to them what they failed to understand.

Encouraging the students to be thorough in their quest of knowledge.

Citing visual examples and tangible similarities to enhance understanding and to deeply entrench it in the mind. This will enable the student to acquire the necessary analytical skills that could be applied in similar situations. Making parallels between two matters does not necessarily mean that they are identical in all aspects. In this case, the believer is not similar or equal, in other aspects, to inanimate objects.

Humility is a recommended trait as long as it does not lead to missing a benefit, for this reason ʿUmar wished that his son had not remained silent.

The ḥadīth highlights a desirable trait; respecting elders which include letting fathers speak ahead of their sons who, also, should restrain themselves even if they thought their understanding is the correct one.

A senior scholar may not understand an issue that is recognised by those who are less versed. Knowledge is bestowed by Allah who gives his gifts to whomever He wills.

Imām Malik observed, based on this ḥadīth, that it is acceptable to have inner thoughts of desire of being praised for good deeds, as long as the ultimate objective is the pleasure of Allah. This is based on ʿUmar's lamenting that his son should have said what he had understood and given the right answer.

Why did ʿUmar wish that? Human nature is built around wishing good for oneself and one's children. ʿUmar wanted his child's brilliance to be known at this tender age, so he may get closer to the Prophet ﷺ who, quite possibly, may pray to Allah to increase his grasp of knowledge as he prayed for ʿAbdullah ibn ʿAbbās when he brought the Prophet ﷺ water to cleanse himself on his own initiative without a request from the Prophet ﷺ who then asked Allah to "give him the insight to Islamic knowledge and teach him the meaning of the Qur'ān." And Ibn ʿAbbās ended as the Prophet ﷺ had wished.

There is nothing to frown upon if a person became pleased when his child is correct in giving the right answer.

The ḥadīth alludes to how ʿUmar did not value much the pleasures of this world; he equalled his son's understanding of one single issue to the high value of a herd of camels of the best qualities (as one narration indicated).

A child will not be reprehended if he, in the presence of a parent, answered about something he knows, even if the parent did not know it. This does not constitute a discourtesy.

The ḥadīth portrays how modest and respectful the Companions were to their elders and seniors and how wary were they to talk in their presence.

The Malikite Imām Ibn Farḥūn cited this ḥadīth in his book 'The Pearl in teaching the elite' *Durratu-l-Ghawwāṣ fī Muḥāḍarati-l-Khawāṣṣ*, commonly known as the Riddles of Ibn Farḥūn. He then reached the conclusion that 'the ḥadīth indicates that a scholar should classify his students by asking them to solve complex riddles to see how good their mental talents are in solving problems and clarifying ambiguities. Scholars of fiqh call these 'riddles', scholars of inheritance call it 'conundrums' and scholars of Arabic grammar call it 'brainteasers.''[105]

Teaching by Analogy and Comparison

At times, the Prophet ﷺ used analogy to explain injunctions and its reasons to his companions when they were confused about its reasoning or unclear about its conclusion. He would clarify obscure or subtle issues through analogy and they would become familiar with the procedures and objectives of the '*Sharīʿa* and would understand its underlying principles.

❖ ḤADĪTH **54:** Bukhārī reported[106] on the authority of Ibn ʿAbbās ؓ that 'A woman from the tribe of Juhaina came to the Prophet ﷺ and said 'My mother pledged that she would perform hajj, but she did not and has now passed away. Should I perform hajj on her behalf?' "Yes." The Prophet ﷺ said, "Perform hajj on her behalf. Tell me, if your mother had a debt that she didn't pay, would you pay it?" She replied, 'Yes.' The Prophet ﷺ said, "Fulfil what is due to Allah, for He is more deserving of getting his dues."'

❖ ḤADĪTH 55: Muslim reported[107] on the authority of Abū Dharr al-Ghifārī ؓ that, 'some of the companions of the Prophet ﷺ said to the Prophet ﷺ 'O Messenger of Allah! The wealthy have reaped all the rewards; they pray as we pray, they fast as we fast and they give charity from their vast wealth.' He replied, "Has not Allah made for you what you can give in charity? Every glorification *Tasbīḥ* of Allah counts as a charity. Every exaltation of Allah *Takbīr* counts as a charity. Every praise of Allah *Taḥmīd* counts as a charity. Every declaration of the oneness of Allah *Tahlīl* counts as a charity. Advocating goodness counts as a charity. Countering evil counts as a charity. Even making love to one's spouse counts as a charity." The companions wondered, 'O Messenger of Allah! When we enjoy ourselves will we be rewarded?!' The Prophet said, "Tell me, if it was done unlawfully, wouldn't it count as a sin? Likewise, if it is done lawfully it will be rewarded."

The Prophet ﷺ used rational analogy to compare the two issues until it became clear to them and they discerned what they did not observe earlier; that lawful pleasure is rewarded because of its good and desirable consequences. The Prophet ﷺ termed as "charity" deeds such as praising and thanking Allah, as these are the metaphorical counterpart of the monetary charity that the wealthy bestow upon their less fortunate brothers for the sake of Allah. Both will lead to rewards from Allah.

❖ ḤADĪTH 56: Abū Dāwūd, Tirmidhī, al-Nasā'ī and Ibn Mājah

reported[108] on the authority of Saʿd ibn Abī Waqqāṣ ﷺ who said, 'I heard the Prophet ﷺ being asked about selling dry dates in exchange for fresh ones. He asked those around him, "Do fresh dates weigh less when they get dry?" They replied, 'Yes.' So he prohibited that.' It goes without saying that the Prophet ﷺ knew fully that fresh dates weigh less when they get dry, for he lived in the heart of the Arabian Peninsula, the land of dry and fresh dates and this is something that is known to even its most ignorant people. However, the Prophet ﷺ asked "Do fresh dates weigh less when they get dry?" to draw the attention of his companions, listeners and followers to the reason for prohibiting the sale of dry dates in exchange for fresh ones, which is that they weigh less when they get dry and as such the deal was a fair deal based on equal weight. He indicated expressly the reason for the injunction since it may not be clear to the companions, which became a standard rule in all transactions.

Teaching by examples and proverbs

Very often the Prophet ﷺ sought to explain what he meant by citing tangible examples that people could see with their own eyes, taste with their tongues, could easily perceive and touch with their hands. This method facilitates comprehension for the student enabling him quickly to grasp fully what he is being taught or forewarned against.

The scholars of linguistic styles would concur that using figurative examples plays a major role in clarifying ambiguities and displaying intricacies. Allah has set forth numerous examples and parables in his great Book, the Qur'ān and the Prophet ﷺ followed the Qur'ān in this regards and extensively used examples in his sermons, speeches and forewarning. Some scholars of ḥadīth collected proverbs that came in the ḥadīths of the Prophet ﷺ such as Abū-l-Ḥasan al-ʿAskarī (d. 310 AH), Abū Aḥmad al-ʿAskarī (d. 382 AH), Judge Abū Muḥammad al-Ḥasan ibn ʿAbdur Raḥmān ibn ar-Rāmahurmuzī (d. 360 AH). The books of ḥadīth have many ḥadīths that would fall under this category, from which I shall quote a few examples:

❖ ḤADĪTH 57: Abū Dāwūd reported[109] on the authority of Anas ﷺ who said, 'the Messenger of Allah ﷺ said, "The example of the believer who recites the Qur'ān is the example of the citron *Citrus medica* (or Adam's apple); its fragrance is nice and its taste is good. The example of the believer who does not recite the Qur'ān is like the example of the date; it tastes good but has no fragrance. The example of the sinner who recites the Qur'ān is like the example of basil; its smell is nice but its taste is bitter. The example of the sinner who does not recite the Qur'ān is like the example of the bitter apple *Citrullus Colocynth*; its taste is bitter and it has no fragrance.

The example of the righteous companion is that of a perfumer; if you get no perfume from him, you will get the smell of a nice fragrance. The example of the corrupt companion is that of an iron smith at the bellows; if you missed his soot, you will get his smoke."

The first example establishes the distinctions the believer enjoys and the high merits of his deeds. It exposes the despicable level of the sinner and the corruptness of his deeds.

These vivid examples that the Prophet ﷺ gave are very effective in promoting goodness and strongly forewarning against evil, using easy-to-understand methods. He used them to encourage us to be keen on accompanying the pious and the scholars and to attend their gatherings, as it will bring us good in this life and hereafter.

The Prophet ﷺ used it to forewarn us to steer away from the company of evil doers and sinners.

Ibn Qayyim said, 'The Prophet, in this ḥadīth, divided people into four categories: (1) Believers who recite the Qur'ān: the best of people, (2) Believers who do not recite the Qur'ān: below the first category, but both are fortunate, (3) those who recite the Qur'ān without faith in their hearts: they are the hypocrites and (4) those who neither recite the Qur'ān nor believe. These two categories are the wretched ones. Belief and the Qur'ān is the light that Allah blesses the hearts of his followers with and they are the basis of every good in this world and in the hereafter. Their study is the best and the most virtuous knowledge. In fact, no other knowledge can truly benefit a person like the knowledge of the Qur'ān and Belief.'[110]

❖ ḤADĪTH 58: Bukhārī and Muslim reported on the authority of Abū Mūsā al-ᶜAshᶜarī ﷺ who said that the Prophet ﷺ said, "The example of what Allah sent me with of guidance and knowledge is like that of generous rain that fell on a land. A part of that land was good and unpolluted; it absorbed the water and brought up a great deal of silage and grass. Another part was barren but it held the water and Allah benefited people with it as they drank, irrigated their crops and planted new ones. The rain fell on another part that was flat and it neither held any water nor did it grow silage. The first is the example of those who studied and learned the religion of Allah and Allah benefited them with what Allah sent me with to learn and teach. The other is the example of those who did pay the slightest heed and did not accept the guidance of Allah that I have been sent with."[111]

Abū-l-ᶜAbbās Aḥmad al-Qurṭubī, a Malikite scholar of ḥadīth, said in his commentary on *Ṣaḥīḥ* that, 'The Prophet ﷺ described his religion as a rain that fell on a large area when people needed it most, for this was the condition of humanity before the Prophet ﷺ came with his message and just as a rain brings life to a dead land, the knowledge of Islam revives a dead heart. Then he compared those who heard his talks to different soils that rain falls on. There are those who understood his teaching and practiced it like a good fertile soil absorbs water and brings benefit through plants and crops.

There are those who focus on gathering knowledge and spend all their time on that, but they don't follow it entirely or do not truly understand it; they are like a soil that collects water in ponds and benefits people with it. Those are whom the Prophet ﷺ meant in his other ḥadīth "May Allah brighten a person who heard my speech, memorised it and then conveyed it exactly as he had heard it. For a person may convey knowledge but he is not knowledgeable, though he may convey knowledge to someone who will understand it better than him." And there are those who hear the knowledge but do not memorize it, practise it, or convey it to others. They are like a peaty land that does not hold water and it even renders it useless for other soils.

The Prophet ﷺ combined the first two commendable categories together since they both bring about benefit. He singled out the third culpable category as it brings no benefit. And Allah knows best.'[112]

Imām Ibn al-Qayyim elaborated on this in his book[113] '*al-Wābil aṣ-Ṣayyib min al-Kalim aṭ-Ṭayyib* The laden rain from the good word', 'The first category are people who convey knowledge and understand it, promote its practice and implement it as well. The second category are people who convey knowledge, observe it and practice it and understand it reasonably. The third category are unfortunate people who do not convey knowledge or understand it, let alone observing it and could not care less about learning or understanding it. They have not accepted the guidance of Allah nor felt its importance. Rather, they have turned away from it.'

Imām Nawawī, in his Commentary on Muslim[114], said, 'This ḥadīth contains various kinds of knowledge; using parables, praising learning and teaching and encouraging them strongly and censuring those who turn their back on knowledge.'

❖ ḤADĪTH 59: Bukhārī and Tirmidhī reported[115] on the authority of an-Nuʿmān ibn Bashīr ﷺ who said, 'The Prophet ﷺ said, "The likeness of those who observe the limits set by Allah, those who cross it and those who do not fulfill it is that of a group that shared a ship, some of them went to the lower deck and others to the upper deck. To obtain water, those who were in the lower deck had to pass by those who were above and thus annoyed them. A person from the lower deck therefore took an axe and started cutting at the bottom of the ship. Those on the upper deck came to him and asked him, 'What are you doing?' He replied, 'I annoyed you and I must get water.' If they hold him; they and he, will be saved. If they let him continue; they and he, will be doomed."'

Those who wanted to drill a hole in the ship are like those who transgress the limits set by Allah. Those who did not join them are of two groups: Those who stopped them and they are the guardians of the limits set by Allah. Or those who kept silent and they compromised the limits set by Allah.

Thus, the ḥadīth indicates that observing the laws of Allah would protect those who applied it and those on whom it was applied. Otherwise, both will be destroyed; the wrongdoer because of his deed and the one who kept silent because of his tacit acceptance.

The ḥadīth indicates that commanding others to observe Allah's orders is a duty that is punishable if neglected.

It also shows that a scholar may use a metaphor to explain a rule. One should exercise patience over the harm caused by a neighbour if encountering it may lead to more harmful results.[116]

❖ ḤADĪTH 60: Imām Nasā'ī reported[117] that Ibn ʿUmar ﷺ narrated that the Messenger of Allah ﷺ said, "The example of the hypocrite is like a sheep going from one flock to another. Once here and then there – undecided on which one to follow."

Sometimes the Prophet ﷺ, in illustrating a meaning, would resort to drawing on the ground and in the sand as Imām Aḥmad reported in his Musnad on the authority of Jābir and Ibn 'Masʿūd (may Allah be pleased with both of them). Also, Abū ʿAbdullah al-Marwazī reported this in his book, as-Sunnah, on the authority of Jābir and Ibn ʿAbbās (may Allah be pleased with both of them)[118]:

❖ ḤADĪTH 61: Jābir ﷺ said, 'We were sitting with the Prophet ﷺ, when he drew on the ground with his hand a line like this in front of him. He then said, "This is the path of Allah, Mighty and Glorious is He." He then drew two lines to the right and two lines to the left and said, "These are the paths of Satan." He then placed his hand on the centre line and recited this verse, "This is my straight path; follow it and do not follow other paths that would take you away from the path of Allah. That He has enjoined upon you so that you may continuously be God concious."'[119]

❖ ḤADĪTH 62: Bukhārī reported[120] on the authority of ʿAbdullah ibn Masʿūd ﷺ who said, 'The Prophet ﷺ drew a square. He then drew a vertical line across its centre and beyond its top. He then drew small lines on either side in the middle of this line. He then said, "This is man, this is his lifespan encompassing him and the line protruding out of the square is his long hopes. These small lines are the events of life. If one misses him, another will get to him. If this missed him, the next will hit him. If all missed him, old-age will catch up with him."' The Messenger ﷺ explained by what he drew on the sand how the long hopes of humans are interrupted by sudden death, debilitating illnesses and ailments, or by old-age. He, implicitly, directed them to curb their hopes and to prepare for sudden death. As we have seen, he used sand on the ground to explain this.

❖ ḤADĪTH **63:** Imām Aḥmad reported in his Musnad[121] on the authority of ʿAbdullah ibn ʿAbbās (may Allah be pleased with both of them) who said, 'The Messenger of Allah ﷺ drew four lines on the ground and then asked, "Do you know why I drew these lines?" The companions replied, 'Allah and His messenger know best.' Then the Messenger of Allah ﷺ replied, "The best women of the people of paradise are Khadīja bint Khuwaylid, Fāṭima bint Muḥammad, Maryam bint ʿImrān and Āsiya bint Muzāḥim, the wife of Pharaoh."'

I could not trace anyone who explained the reason behind the Prophet drawing these four lines to reveal the merit of these four women. It appears to me and Allah knows best, that the most probable reason is to emphasise visually to the companions the ranking of these fine ladies after having heard it from the mouth of the Prophet.

Combining speech and movement in teaching

At times, the Prophet ﷺ would combine, when teaching, speech with hand movements to clarify his point and stress the importance of what he was saying or teaching to those present.

❖ ḤADĪTH **64:** Muslim and Bukhārī (and the text is his), reported[122] that Abū Mūsā al-Ashʿarī ﷺ said, 'The Messenger of Allah ﷺ said, "A believer to another believer is like a building

- strengthening each other." Then the Messenger of Allah ﷺ interlocked between his fingers."

❖ ḤADĪTH 65: Muslim reported[123] in the lengthy ḥadīth of Jābir ibn ʿAbdullah ﷺ about the ḥajj of the Prophet ﷺ that he said, "If I was able to redo what I have just done, I would not have offered my sacrifice - I would have made it an ʿUmrah. So whoever among you does not have an animal to sacrifice may end his iḥrām and make his ritual an ʿUmrah." Then Surāqah ibn Mālik ibn Ju'shum stood up and said, 'O Messenger of Allah! Is this order only for this year or forever?' The Messenger of Allah ﷺ then interlocked his fingers - one into the other - and said, "The ʿUmrah has been included in the ḥajj, the ʿUmrah has been included in the ḥajj. Indeed forever and ever."

The most obvious meaning of "the ʿUmrah has been included in the ḥajj" is that it refuted the pre-Islamic position that forbade performing ʿUmrah during the months of ḥajj. ʿUmrah can be performed during the months of ḥajj.

❖ ḤADĪTH 66: Bukhārī reported[124] on the authority of Sahl ibn Saʿd as-Sāʿidī ﷺ who said, "The Messenger of Allah ﷺ said, "I and the guardian of the orphan will be in paradise like these two." He then showed his forefinger and middle-finger and left a slight gap between the two.'

❖ ḤADĪTH 67: Bukhārī (the text is his) and Muslim reported[125] a lengthy ḥadīth narrated by Abū Hurayra ﷺ about three infants who spoke in their cradle. The Messenger of Allah ﷺ mentioned them as, "Jesus the son of Mary ﷺ, the infant son of Jurayj, the monk." Then, the Prophet mentioned, "a lady from the Israelites was breastfeeding her child when a handsome rider passed by her. She said, 'O Allah! Make my child like him.' On that the child left her breast and facing the rider said, 'O Allah! Do not make me like him.' The child then went back to suck her breast." Abū Hurayra ﷺ further said, 'As if I'm now looking at the Prophet ﷺ sucking his finger.' "After a while a group passed by dragging, harassing and beating a female slave. The infant's mother said, 'O Allah! Do not make my child like this!' On that the child left her breast and said, 'O Allah! Make me like her.' 'Why is that?' She asked and the child replied, 'The rider is a terrible tyrant while they were accusing the maid of theft and fornication and she just responded saying, 'Allah is sufficient for me and he is the Best Protector!'"

❖ ḤADĪTH **68:** Imām Aḥmad reported in his Musnad[126] on the authority of ʿAbdullah ibn Masʿūd ﷺ who said, 'Once we were sitting with the Messenger of Allah ﷺ in the company of about eighty men of Quraysh. Every one of them belonged to the Quraysh. And by Allah I never saw more handsome faces than theirs. They brought up the subject of women and spoke about them and the Prophet joined them till I wished that he would stop. Then, I approached him. And he pronounced the Shahāda and then said, "O Quraysh! You are leaders as long as you do not disobey Allah, Exalted is He. But if you disobey Him, He will send you someone who will fend you off just as this twig is peeled off." – waving a twig that was in his hand. He then peeled it and it appeared shining white.'

❖ ḤADĪTH **69:** Muslim and Tirmidhī (the text is his) reported on the authority of Sufyān ibn ʿAbdullah ath-Thaqafī ﷺ who said, 'I said, 'O Messenger of Allah! Tell me something I could hold on to.' He replied, "Say: My Sustainer is Allah and then adhere to that." I said, 'O Messenger of Allah! What is thing you most fear for me?' The Messenger of Allah ﷺ held his own tongue and said, "This!"'

❖ ḤADĪTH 70: Muslim and Bukhārī (the text is his) reported[127] on the authority of Ibn ʿAbbās (may Allah be pleased with both of them), 'that the Prophet ﷺ was asked about his ḥajj (on the day of sacrifice), and he was asked, 'I sacrificed before I threw.' The Prophet raised his hand and said, "And there is no harm in that". He was further asked, 'I shaved before I sacrificed.' The Prophet raised his hand and said, "And there is no harm in that".'

❖ ḤADĪTH 71: Muslim reported on the authority of al-Miqdād ibn al-Aswad ؓ, who said, 'I heard the Messenger of Allah ﷺ say, "On the Day of Resurrection, the sun will be brought close to the creation till it is about a mile from them. People will then be surrounded by perspiration proportional to their deeds. There will be those whose perspiration will be up to their ankles. There will be those whose perspiration will be up to their knees. There will be those whose perspiration will up to their hips. There will be those whom perspiration will completely suppress," and the Messenger of Allah ﷺ pointed with his hand to his mouth.'

❖ ḤADĪTH 72: In his book on the additions of Ibn ḥibbān on *Ṣaḥīḥ al-Bukhārī* and *Muslim*, al-Ḥāfiẓ al-Haythamī, reported on the authority of ʿUqbah ibn ʿĀmir ؓ who said, "The Messenger of Allah ﷺ said, "The sun will come close to earth and people will perspire. There will be those whose perspiration will be up to their ankles. There will be those whose perspiration will be up to their knees. There will be those whose perspiration will reach their thighs, those whose perspiration will reach their hips, those whose perspiration will reach their necks and those whose perspiration will reach the middle of their mouths." ʿUqbah moved his hand to cup his mouth. He then said, 'I saw the Messenger of Allah ﷺ doing this. There will be those who will be completely submerged.' He then pointed with his hand above his head.'[128]

At times, the Prophet ﷺ would carry in his hand an item he had just prohibited and show it to his listeners, combining visual demonstration with verbal prohibition, which will reinforce his message and would be more explicit in demonstrating its prohibition and unlawfulness.

❖ ḤADĪTH 73: Abū Dāwūd, Nasā'ī and Ibn Mājah (the text is his) reported[129] on the authority of ʿAlī ibn Abī Ṭālib ﷺ who said, 'The Messenger of Allah ﷺ took a piece of silk in his left hand and some gold in his right hand. He then raised both with his hands and said, "These two are prohibited for the males of my ummah, permitted for their females."'

❖ ḤADĪTH 74: Imām Aḥmad reported in his Musnad on the authority of ʿUbāda ibn aṣ-Ṣāmit ﷺ who said, 'The Prophet ﷺ used to take a hair from a camel of proceeds of war and say, "My share in it is just as the share of anyone of you. Avoid taking something of it by stealth, for those who commit it will be disgraced on the Day of Resurrection. Don't hide even a thread, a needle and whatever is more than that. Struggle in the cause of Allah, Exated is He, whether opposed by those close to you or others far from you and whether you are settled or travelling. Jihād is one of the doors of paradise and through it Allah, Blessed and Exalted is He will relieve distress and worry. Apply penal laws to those who near you as well as those who are not. Do not let the criticism of anyone deviate you from the cause of Allah."'[130]

Initiating teaching without being asked

The Prophet ﷺ frequently would take the initiative and teach his companions even though they did not ask him. He did this particularly when it came to subtle but important issues that one would not discern let alone ask about. Thus, the Prophet ﷺ would teach his companions answers to doubts before they arose, lest they come up and settle in theirs minds, with undesirable effects.

❖ ḤADĪTH 75: Bukhārī and Muslim reported[131] on the authority of Abū Hurayra ؓ who said, 'The Messenger of Allah ﷺ said, "Satan comes to one of you and asks: 'Who created such and such thing?' He continues asking questions till he asks: 'Who created your Lord?' When a person reaches that stage, he should seek refuge in Allah and stop there."'

The Prophet ﷺ directed us not to go along with Satan with such thoughts and to refute him with the help of Allah. We should realise that Satan wants to corrupt our faith and minds by these thoughts and as such we should strive to keep it away and cease such thoughts through meaningful thinking.

Imām al-Khaṭṭābī, commenting on this ḥadīth, said, 'The ḥadīth implies that if Satan whispered such thoughts and we repulsed him through Allah; he will be repulsed. The whispers of Satan never end; every time you refute his argument, he would bring forth another, till he leads you to doubts. However, to ask 'who created your Lord?' is ridiculous and self contradictory. The Creator cannot be created and consequentiality, in this regard, is impossible, as creatures need a creator and if he needed to be created, then he is not the Creator. If one asks what is the problem with the Creator creating himself? He would be told that this is paradoxical; you assumed a creator which means presence first, then said that he created himself which means he was not the first. As the cause precedes the result, then what you say is impossible.

Along these lines Ibn at-Tīn said, 'that if it was possible that a creator would have, in turn, a creator, then that would necessitate consequentiality till we end at the original and eternal creator who initiated all these creatures; Allah, Blessed and Exalted is He.'

Shaikh Muḥammad ʿAbduh, in his book 'The Message of Tawḥīd' illustrated the limitations of the human mind to reach the essence of physical phenomenon let alone to grasp the nature of God. He wrote, 'if we assess the human mind realistically, we'll find the furthest limit of its perfection is to discern the phenomenon of the physical world around it utilising the tools of senses, emotions, or thinking, then the mind will draw conclusions about its origin, patterns and phases. To be truly able to explain a phenomenon in isolation of these criterions is impossible, for that would necessitate reaching its design and the motives of its behaviour, something that humans cannot decipher and the maximum they can reach is to observe its behaviour and effects.

Light, for example, is most obvious in our lives and scientists can explain its behaviour and many effects and patterns, but they cannot explain the essence of light itself and why it happens. God did not make it indispensable for our life to know the essence of things, but we are well equipped to study its properties and phenomenon and we enjoy establishing scientific properties and patterns. To work on reaching the creative mechanism is futile and an inappropriate use of our creative faculties.

To think about the nature of the Creator is beyond the realms of the human mind, which cannot relate to the divine nature. On the other side, it is a wasteful attempt to reach the unattainable and a dangerous slippery slope that could lead to total confusion, as one attempts to define the indefinable and to delineate the omnipresent. Allah, Exated is He said, "Nothing is like him and he is the All-Seeing and the All-Hearing." If we cannot understand our own nature, then it goes without saying that we cannot comprehend the nature of the Creator.

ʿAbdullah al-Nabrāwī, in his commentary on the forty ḥadīth of Nawawī, when dealing with the thirtieth ḥadīth narrated by Abī

Thaʿlaba al-Khushani ؓ who said, the Messenger of Allah ﷺ said, "Indeed Allah, Exalted is He enjoined certain acts; do not neglect it. He set limits; do not cross them. He forbade certain things; do not commit them. He kept silent on certain issues, not because he forgot but because of His mercy for you; so do not search them out." Al-Nabrāwī ؓ said, 'Among the issues we are not required to pursue are articles of faith that relate to the realm of the unseen that we were asked to believe in without knowing its nature. Trying to understand its nature could lead to uncertainty and doubts or end with denial and disbelief and hence came the advice of Ibn Isḥāq, 'We should not reflect upon the nature of the Creator and the creature beyond what Allah specified. If Allah said that, "Indeed, everything sings his praise", one should not ask how stones would praise their Lord? For the Creator, Glorified and Exalted is He, is the One who told us this and can make this praise in any form He wills.

In addition to ḥadīths in Bukhārī, Muslim has ḥadīths that support the forbidding of reflecting on God's nature, "People will continue inquiring till they reach, 'God created creatures, so who created God?' Whoever comes to such a question should say, 'I believe in God.'" I have extensively commented on this side issue because of its utmost importance especially among the young students at their schools.

❖ ḤADĪTH 76: Abū Dāwūd reported[132] on the authority of Abū Hurayra ؓ who said, 'The Messenger of Allah ﷺ said, "People will continue questioning each other until it is said, 'God created creatures, so who created God?' Whoever experiences this should say, 'I believe in Allah.'" In another narration, "When they say that, you should say, 'Allah is One. Allah is the Self-Sufficient. He did not beget anyone nor was He begotten. And there is none similar to Him.' One should then puff three times to his left side and seek refuge from Satan."

To say 'I believe in Allah' is to affirm the resolute faith in the heart with the declaration of the tongue in defiance of Satan.

To say the attribute of Allah mentioned in the second narration, is to rebuff Satan by reiterating that God is the Originator of creation, the One and only God, Self-Sufficient and He is without equal.

To puff, or spit, to the left is to demonstrate disdain for Satan and to dispel his demonic whispers.

We were advised to seek the protection of God and not to reflect and debate as the independence of God of any creator is beyond debate and wading into it will lead nowhere but to loss. As such, the resort to Allah is the safe heaven of the believers.

❖ ḤADĪTH 77: Ibn ḥibbān, in his *Ṣaḥīḥ*[133], cited the following ḥadīth of Anas ibn Mālik ﷺ under the title 'Citing precedents that permit the scholar to ask his students on issues that he is about to teach them and to encourage them to ask such questions', 'that the Messenger of Allah ﷺ came out after midday and led the people in Ẓuhr prayers and when he finished, he stood on the pulpit and spoke about the Hour and mentioned that gigantic events will precede it. He then said, "Whoever wishes to ask me about anything then should do so. By Allah, you will not ask me about anything except that I will inform you about it as long as I am here in my place." Anas ibn Mālik said, 'People cried profusely upon hearing this from the Messenger of Allah ﷺ and the Messenger of Allah ﷺ continued prompting them, "Ask me, ask me!" ʿAbdullah ibn Ḥudhāfa then stood up and asked, 'Who is my father, O Messenger of Allah?' "Your father is Ḥudhāfa," the Prophet answered.'

❖ ḤADĪTH 78: Bukhārī and Muslim (the text is his) also reported[134] the previous ḥadīth on the authority of Anas ﷺ 'that the Messenger of Allah ﷺ came out after midday and led them in Ẓuhr prayer. When he finished, he stood on the pulpit and spoke about the Hour and also mentioned that gigantic events will precede it. He then said, "Whoever wishes to ask me about anything should do so, for by Allah, you will not ask me about anything except that I will inform you about it as long as I am here in this place of mine."

Anas said, 'People cried profusely upon hearing that from the Messenger of Allah ﷺ and the Messenger of Allah ﷺ continued prompting them, "Ask me, ask me!" ʿAbdullah ibn Ḥudhāfa stood up and asked, 'Who is my father, O Messenger of Allah?' "Your father is Ḥudhāfa," the Prophet answered.

When the Messenger of Allah ﷺ continued saying, "Ask me, ask me!" ʿUmar sat down and said, 'We are pleased with Allah as our Lord, Islam as the religion and Muḥammad as the Messenger.' The Messenger of Allah ﷺ then fell silent when ʿUmar said this, then the Messenger of Allah ﷺ said, "By the One Who my life is in His hand, I was just been shown paradise and hell across this wall and I never seen good and evil like this day."'

The reason for the crying of the people, as revealed in other narrations, is that the Prophet ﷺ became clearly angry when the people started asking too many questions including some silly ones like, 'Where is my lost camel? Should we perform Hajj every year? Where I will end? etc...' When they saw his anger, which was calm and within reason, they started crying fearing the punishment of Allah.

The reason that ʿAbdullah ibn Ḥudhāfa as-Sahmī asked the Prophet ﷺ, about his father, is that in pre-Islamic days *Jāhiliyya*, people when in a heated argument would disparage each other about who truly their father was. ʿAbdullah was annoyed with this as explained in another ḥadīth of Anas ﷺ reported by Bukhārī.

It is appropriate to give here a brief biography of this great companion; ʿAbdullah ibn Ḥudhāfa. He was one of the wise, courageous, honourable people among the companions. He belonged to the tribe of Quraysh. He and his mother were among the early Muslims. He emigrated to Abyssinia with his brother Qays and some historians say he attended the battle of Badr.

The Prophet ﷺ appointed him as the leader of a taskforce and also sent him as a messenger to Khosrau inviting him to Islam. Khosrau tore the letter and when ʿAbdullah told the Prophet ﷺ, he said, "May God tear up his kingdom" and he said, "If Khosrau dies; he will be the last king." Sherveh, the son of Khosrau assassinated him soon after.

In the year 19 AH, he was among an army that ʿUmar dispatched to fight the Byzantines. ʿAbdullah was captured and taken, as a prisoner of war to the Emperor. The Emperor offered ʿAbdullah a fiefdom if he became a Christian and when he refused, he ordered him to be put on a cross and shot with arrows. When that did not scare him he was shown another prisoner of war being thrown into a fiercely heated cauldron with boiling water that caused the prisoner's flesh to sizzle and soon his bones could be seen. He was threatened with the same fate if he did not convert to Christianity. As he was being taken away he began to cry and the Emperor ordered him back and asked him, 'Why did you weep?' 'I cried,' said ʿAbdullah, 'because I wished I have a hundred souls to have all of them thrown into this pot for the sake of God.'

The emperor was incredulous and told him, 'Kiss my forehead and I will set you free.' 'No!' Said ʿAbdullah and the Emperor said, 'Kiss my forehead and I'll free you and all the Muslim prisoners.' ʿAbdullah kissed his forehead and the Emperor freed eighty Muslims who came with ʿAbdullah to ʿUmar in Madina who was very pleased and said, 'Every Muslim should kiss the forehead of ʿAbdullah and I shall be the first.'

ʿAbdullah participated in the conquering of Egypt, died there and was buried in Cairo. He was a fun-loving person. One time he untied the belt holding the saddle of the camel of the Prophet ﷺ who almost fell and apparently was amused.

The version of Muslim on the authority of ʿUbayd Allah ibn ʿUtbah elaborated more, 'The mother of ʿAbdullah ibn Ḥudhāfa said to her son, 'I have never heard of a more disobedient son! Weren't you worried that your mother committed one of the sins prevailing among women in the pre-Islamic days? What a disgrace to her before everyone that would be?' ʿAbdullah ibn Ḥudhāfa replied, 'By Allah, had the Prophet linked me to a black slave, I would have accepted him.'

When the Prophet ﷺ said more and more, "Ask me, ask me!" ʿUmar sat down on his knees and said, 'O Messenger of Allah! We are pleased with Allah as our Lord, Islam as the religion and Muḥammad as the Messenger.' The Prophet fell silent and then said, "By Allah in whose hands lay my life, I was just shown paradise and hell across this wall and I never seen good and evil like this."'

One must reflect on the unshaken faith that ʿAbdullah had in the trustworthiness of the Prophet ﷺ. The story may imply that ʿAbdullah was of a white complexion, since in emphasis one tends to use extreme contrast, i.e. black vs. white.

Teaching through answers of questions

The Prophet ﷺ was always available to answer the questions of his companions and through these answers he taught many laws, injunctions and fundamentals of religion. He encouraged his companions not to hesitate to ask questions on situations and problems that worried them or on what they needed to know of appropriate rules and regulations.

❖ ḤADĪTH 79: Abū Dāwūd reported[135] on the authority of Jābir ﷺ that the Prophet ﷺ said, "Asking is the only cure of ignorance."

This ḥadīth is a reflection of the order of Allah in the Qur'ān, "Ask the people of knowledge if you do not know."

It must be noted that the Qur'ānic and ḥadīth texts that discourage asking questions are construed to discourage asking needless or trivial questions, or that pertain to the unseen that faith requires us to accept. We are also discouraged to ask too many trivial questions about unimportant issues while neglecting learning issues and rituals of prime importance. Likewise, we should not ask questions if our aim is not truth and knowledge but argument and arrogance.

I would like here to quote Imām ash-Shāṭibī in his great book 'The Convergence *al-Muwāfaqāt*' where he listed categories of questions and the rules pertaining to each category:

A question may come from a scholar or a student and the person they are asking either knows the answer or doesn't and as such we have four categories:

The first is a scholar who is asking a question. This could be divided into six subcategories: to review the conclusion, to dispel a misunderstanding, to memorise an issue lest he forgets it, to mask, in his question, an error that needs correction, to ask on behalf of present learners, or to catch up what he may have missed.

The learner is asking another learner. This could be divided into four subcategories: comparing notes, asking him about what he didn't hear, doing exercises before meeting the scholar, or seeking his explanation to what the scholar has taught.

The scholar is asking the leaner. This could be divided into four subcategories: to point out an ambiguity that needs clarification, to probe the extent of his knowledge, to seek his understanding if he was of a sharp mind, or to highlight for him what he has just learned and how to apply it in other cases.

The learner is asking the scholar so he can learn what he does not know. The first three categories always deserve an answer unless there is a very compelling reason. Otherwise, one should admit that he does not know the answer.

Answering the fourth category is not a must and it is subject to certain qualifications. One should answer if the scholar is knowledgeable about the topic and the question is necessary to the learner and he is capable of understanding the issues and applying the answer. The answer should not lead to undue burdens or further arguments. The scholar may decline to answer if he felt the question was unnecessary. Answering questions may even become inadvisable if it came from a person who cannot understand or appreciate the answer or who was seeking controversy.

The companions of the Prophet ﷺ came to him seeking answers and clarification to their questions and ambiguities so that they fully understood, practiced and increased their faith. The Prophet ﷺ would answer each with what would bring comfort and satisfaction. The books of ḥadīth provide us with so many rich replies of the Prophet ﷺ to the religious questions of his companions. I have cited some already and will cite some more in the following paragraphs.

❖ ḤADĪTH **80:** Muslim reported[136] on the authority of an-Nawwās ibn Simʿān al-Kilābī who said, 'I remained with the Messenger of Allah ﷺ in Medina for a year without making it my home just to be able to ask the Prophet, for once one of us emigrated he would not ask the Messenger of Allah ﷺ anything. So I asked him about good and evil and he ﷺ replied, "Good is to have good manners. Evil is what goes in your mind but you dislike that people discover it."'

It seems that there was a tradition among the people of Medina that didn't favour asking the Prophet ﷺ something that was quite normal for visitors of Medina. This is why companions lived in Medina as a visitor, in order to be able to continue to ask the Prophet ﷺ about various religious issues. The residents of Medina would be pleased when a visitor, specially a bedouin, would ask the Prophet ﷺ a question since they were tolerated for bothering the Prophet ﷺ with their many questions which not infrequently would also be of an interest to the residents. This is evident in the ḥadīth, previously cited, of Anas 'We were pleased when a wise bedouin would come to the Prophet ﷺ and ask him while we are listening.'

The residents of Medina were not prohibited from inquiring about what they needed to know of religious issues, but they hesitated, out of respect, to ask the Prophet ﷺ unless there was a real need. This is clear as books of ḥadīth cite many instances when the Prophet ﷺ was asked by the residents of Medina like the one reported by Muslim[137] on the authority of Abū Hurayra ؓ that, 'The Prophet ﷺ said, "Ask me," but they were too shy to ask till a man came and sat at his knees and said, 'O Messenger of Allah, what is Islam?' In another ḥadīth, Ibn Abā Mulaika said that ʿĀ'isha ؓ used to question anything she heard if she could not understand it and she narrated that one time the Prophet ﷺ said that in the Day of Judgement, "whoever is questioned will be punished," she said, 'I asked, 'Doesn't Allah say, "Then he who is given his record in his right hand; his account will be an easy reckoning[138]"' She said the Prophet ﷺ explained, "That is the review of the record, but if one is questioned then he is doomed."'

Ḥāfiẓ Ibn Ḥajar, in his Commentary on this ḥadīth in Bukhārī, said, 'The ḥadīth clarifies that such questions are not covered by what the companions were discouraged to ask when Allah said, "O you who believe, do not ask about issues that, if revealed to you, will displease you." Ibn Ḥajar continued, 'There were people other than ʿĀ'isha ﷺ who asked the Prophet ﷺ. His wife ḥafṣa, for example, heard him saying, "Those who attended Badr and Hudaibiya will not enter hell." She said, 'Doesn't Allah say "every one of you shall enter it." And another verse was pointed out to her, "Then, we save those who feared their Lord away from punishment."'

Thus, it is for those asking questions just to be difficult whereupon came the discouragement in the Qur'ān, "But those in whose hearts is perversity follow the part thereof that is allegorical, seeking discord and searching for its hidden meanings, but no one knows its hidden meanings except Allah."

The Arabic word *Birr,* as scholars said, means concern, kindness, charity and agreement, all which are the basic elements of good manners.

Not everything that goes in our minds and we hate people to know about it is evil. It is those acts that we have qualms about and we hate that our dear and respected ones knows about. It does not cover our living preferences such as riding or eating. We usually have qualms about things that we know are wrong and of undesirable consequences. This ḥadīth is considered amongst the succinct important ḥadīths.

❖ ḤADĪTH **81:** Muslim and Abū Dāwūd (the text is his) reported on the authority of Ibn ʿAbbās (may Allah, Exalted is He be pleased with both of them) who said, 'The Messenger of Allah ﷺ sent a man from the tribe of Aslam with eighteen camels [to distribute its meat among the poor of Mecca]. He asked the Messenger of Allah ﷺ, 'What if any of these camels is too sick to walk?' He replied, "Slaughter it and then mark it [for the poor] by dipping a shoe in its blood and striking it on both sides and do not eat from it or any of your companions."'

❖ ḤADĪTH 82: Bukhārī and Muslim reported[139] on the authority of Rāfʿi ibn Khadīj who said, I said, 'O Messenger of Allah! We are concerned that tomorrow we'll fight the enemy and we have no knives with us.' He replied, "As long as blood was drained and the name of Allah was mentioned, then eat. But avoid cutting with teeth and claws. I will tell you, as for teeth, they are bones. And as for claws, they are the knives of the Abyssinians."'

This ḥadīth established, through the question and the full answer, the prohibition of the pre-Islamic practice of slaughtering birds and other small animals like rabbits with animal teeth and claws.

❖ ḤADĪTH 83: Muslim, Abū Dāwūd, Nasā'ī, Tirmidhī, Ibn Mājah and Bukhārī (the text is his) reported on the authority of Abū Thaʿlaba al-Khushanī ؓ who said, 'I came to the Prophet ﷺ and said, 'O Messenger of Allah! We live among the People of the Book - can we eat from their utensils? And we live in a hunting area where I hunt with my bow using my untrained dog and my trained hunting dog. So what is suitable for me?' The Prophet replied, "As regards what you said about being among the People of the Book, you should not eat from their utensils except if you have no alternative, then wash it and eat from it. As regards what you said about being in a hunting area, whatever you hunt with your bow while saying the name of Allah, you may eat. Whatever you hunt with your trained hunting dog while saying the name of Allah, you may eat. Whatever you hunt with your untrained dog and you catch up [while still alive] and slaughter; you may eat."

The version of Abū Dāwūd is as follows, 'O Messenger of Allah! We are the neighbours of the People of the Book. They cook pork in their pots and drink alcohol in their utensils.' The Messenger of Allah ﷺ replied, "If you find other than them [pots and utensils] eat and drink from them. But if you find no alternative, wash it thoroughly with water and then eat and drink from it."' Abū Thaʿlaba and his tribe Banī Khushain were among the Arabs living in Syria and hence his questions and the explained answers of the Prophet ﷺ.

Ibn Ḥajar in his Commentary said, 'From this ḥadīth we learn that one may come with all his questions at once to get it answered in details one by one envisaging all possibilities.'

Replying an answer beyond the question

At times, the Prophet ﷺ would answer a person beyond his question if he felt that he needs to know more beyond his question, a trait that shows his perfect kindness and the thorough interest in propagating knowledge.

❖ ḤADĪTH **84:** Imām Mālik and Abū Dāwūd reported[140] on the authority of Abū Hurayra ﷺ who said, 'A person from the tribe of Banī Mudlij asked the Prophet ﷺ, 'O Messenger of Allah! We sail upon the sea carrying with us little water, which if we were to make ablution *Wuḍū'* with, soon we will become thirsty. Can we make ablution with sea water?' The Messenger of Allah ﷺ replied, "Its water purifies and its dead [animals] could be eaten."'

Here the Prophet ﷺ answered this Mudlijite sailor on making ablution with the sea water by telling him that its water is untainted and that ablution with it is valid. The Prophet ﷺ then showed his consideration to this sailor lest he becomes confused about whether he is allowed to eat dead fish something that he may experience while at sea. The Prophet ﷺ therefore explained that it is lawful to eat dead animals of the sea and to benefit from it. The Prophet ﷺ therefore elaborated further on the question by saying, "And its dead [animals] could be eaten."

This elaboration of the answer is very important because it

stated the purity of sea water despite the deaths that occur in it and stated the lawfulness of all marine animals that die in it. This information is essential for the sailor as he may need to eat such dead animals at some time – whether by choice or out of necessity. After this, he can eat it and store it without any qualm. This explanation of the Prophet ﷺ is the essence of goodness in the methods of teaching and providing all that the learner needs.

❖ ḤADĪTH 85: Muslim, Abū Dāwūd and al-Nasā'ī reported[141] on the authority of Ibn ʿAbbās (may Allah be pleased with both of them) who said, 'A woman raised her son, whilst performing ḥajj and she asked, 'O Messenger of Allah! Does ḥajj count for this?' He replied, "Yes. And for you there is reward."'

The scholars said that this ḥadīth indicates the validity of the ḥajj of a small child and that Allah will reward children for acts of worship even if it was not required of them. Such ḥajj will not be considered as fulfilling the ḥajj that is incumbent on adults but will be considered a voluntary ḥajj.

The Prophet ﷺ, in this ḥadīth, replied beyond the question of the woman. She had asked about the validity of her son's ḥajj and he replied affirmatively adding that she also will be rewarded since she is looking after the child. This is an implicit praise of her benevolence and a strong incentive for mothers and fathers of future generations to follow her example in taking, despite difficulties, their young children for the pilgrimage to the sacred House of Allah in order to embed in their hearts and memories the magnificence of the scenes of ḥajj and to ingrain in their souls the greatness of the fifth pillar of Islam. The sight of small children around the Kaʿba moves hearts and souls and spurs tears of reflection and piety.

Deflecting the question

At times, for some great wisdom, the Prophet ﷺ would deflect the question and turn the attention of the questioner away from what he had actually asked.

❖ ḤADĪTH 86: Bukhārī and Muslim reported[142] on the authority of Anas ﷺ that, 'a man said to the Messenger of Allah ﷺ, 'When is the Hour, O Messenger of Allah?' "What have you prepared for it?" The Prophet replied and the man said, 'I have not prepared for it many prayers, fasts and acts of charitiy. However, I love Allah and His messenger.' The Prophet said, "You will be with whom you love."' The Prophet ﷺ turned the questioner away from the time of the Resurrection, which only Allah knows and focused his attention on something else that he needs more and of a greater benefit to him; to prepare for the Resurrection with good deeds.

The Prophet ﷺ elaborated in his answer that a person will be resurrected among those whom he loved and enjoyed company, this is also a forewarning about befriending the unrighteous as that is liable to get us with them in the Hereafter.

This style of deflecting questions is known as 'wisdom style' whereby the answer to a question is moved into a different direction that is more important or beneficial than a straight answer.

❖ ḤADĪTH 87: Bukhārī and Muslim reported on the authority of Ibn ʿUmar (may Allah be pleased with both of them), 'that a person asked the Prophet ﷺ, 'O Messenger of Allah! What can a *muḥrim* (a person performing ḥajj or ʿUmrah) wear?' The Messenger of Allah ﷺ replied, "He should not wear a shirt, a turban, pants, or a burnoose. Nor should he wear clothing that has been dyed with Turmeric[143] or saffron. If he does not have sandals, he may wear leather socks. But he should cut them so that they are below the ankles."

Here we see the Prophet ﷺ was asked about what a person could wear when he is performing ʿUmrah or ḥajj, but the Prophet ﷺ, in his answer, spelled out what should not be worn, which in itself instructs to what should be worn. Since this injunction concerns prohibited types of dresses, it would be more logical to list that instead of enumerating the endless possibilities of what could worn. The Prophet ﷺ therefore specified what is limited to give a practical and concise reply, for if he was to enumerate all that could be worn, it will take too long and will be difficult to remember and apply.

In addition, the Prophet ﷺ explained to him the ruling on wearing leather socks when sandals are not available, which is part of the question albeit in the case of necessity. Thus Prophet ﷺ said to him, "If he does not have sandals, he may wear leather socks. But he should cut them so that they are below the ankles."

❖ ḤADĪTH **88:** Bukhārī and Muslim (the text is his) reported[144] on the authority of Abū Mūsā al-Ashʿarī ﷺ, 'that a bedouin came to the Prophet ﷺ and said, 'O Messenger of Allah! A person fights for war booty, another fights for fame, another fights to show off. Which of these is fighting in the cause of Allah?' The Messenger of Allah ﷺ replied, "Whoever fought to raise high the word of Allah; then that is in the cause of Allah."

In this ḥadīth the Prophet ﷺ did not answer each of the cases of the question and opted for an answer that addresses the essence of the issue; pure intentions and motives.

Scholars listed this brief answer of the Prophet ﷺ among the gems of ḥadīth. If the Prophet ﷺ said, "No. All of this is not for the sake of Allah." We may have considered all other situations to be for the sake of Allah, which obviously is not true. Thus the Prophet ﷺ opted to use this all-encompassing statement to leave no illusions about the motives.

As each of these motives could be praised or censured based on their primary motive, the Prophet ﷺ did not respond by saying yes or no, instead he turned the bedouin's attention to the prime motive. Ibn Ḥajar, in his Commentary, said, 'If the primary motive was raising the word of Allah, these secondary feelings are not important. What is of concern is to participate for motives other than raising the word of Allah. This is confirmed by a ḥadīth reported by Abū Dāwūd on the authority of ʿAbdullah ibn Hawala, 'The Messenger of Allah ﷺ sent us, as infantry, on a task in the hope we will win something from the enemy, but we returned empty-handed. The Prophet ﷺ said, "O Allah, do not put me in charge of them as I might not be able to look after them and do not let them be on their own as they may not be able to look after themselves on their own."'

We learn from this ḥadīth that a student may ask for the underlying reason of a particular ruling, since the bedouin asked, 'Which of these is fighting in the cause of Allah?'

Muslims must acquire knowledge before commencing a deed, so that the deed is sanctioned and guided by the *Sharīʿa*.

CONFIRMING THE QUESTION TO ENSURE A COMPREHENSIVE REPLY

At times, the Prophet ﷺ would ask a person to reiterate his question, although the Prophet ﷺ fully understood it, in order to teach him further, to qualify an answer, or explain it fully.

❖ ḤADĪTH 89: Nasāʾī and Muslim (the text is his) reported[145] on the authority of Abū Qatāda ؓ, 'that the Messenger of Allah addressed them and told them that, "Jihād for the cause of Allah and belief in Allah are the most virtuous deeds." A man stood up and asked, 'O Messenger of Allah! What if I was killed in the cause of Allah; will this pardon my sins?' The Messenger of Allah ﷺ told him, "Yes. If you are killed for the cause of Allah while you are steadfast, pursuing no personal gains, charging and not fleeing." Then the Messenger of Allah ﷺ said, "How did you express it?" The man said, 'If I was killed for the cause of Allah; will this pardon my sins?' The Messenger of Allah ﷺ said, "Yes. If you are killed for the cause of Allah while you are steadfast, pursuing no personal gains, charging and not fleeing unless you owe unpaid debts, for Jibrīl just told me that."'

The debt that the Prophet ﷺ meant here is a debt that one has no intention of repaying. Debt, in this context, is an example of what one may owe to his fellow humans, for a debtor is not worse than a criminal, an embezzler, a traitor, or a thief, etc... The Prophet ﷺ, by highlighting debt, drew attention to all rights due to our fellow humans and that it will not be pardoned by even Jihād and martyrdom for the cause of Allah and other lesser good deeds. Jihād and martyrdom will attain a pardon of the duties one may owe to Allah.

In the narration of Nasā'ī, the Prophet ﷺ said, "Yes. Except debts as Jibrīl whispered this to me just now." So, the Prophet ﷺ asked for the question again to qualify his answer in the light of what Jibrīl told him.

Referring a question to a companion

The Prophet ﷺ, at times, would refer the answer of a question to one of his companions to train him to address similar issues.

❖ ḤADĪTH 90: Bukhārī, Muslim, Abū Dāwūd, Tirmidhī and Ibn Mājah reported[146] on the authority of Ibn ʿAbbās (may Allah be pleased with both of them) who said, 'Abū Hurayra used to relate that a person came to the Messenger of Allah ﷺ upon his return from [the battle of] Uḥud and said, 'Last night I saw a dream, there was a cloud from which butter and honey were dripping. I saw the people scooping it with their palms; some a lot and some a little. And I saw a rope stretching out from heaven to earth and I saw you, O Messenger of Allah, holding onto it and ascending. Another person took hold of it after you and ascended and after him another person took hold of it and ascended. Thereafter, another person took hold of it and it broke off. The rope was then joined for him and he ascended.'

Abū Bakr said, 'O Meseenger of Allah! May my father and mother be your protection, by Allah you shall permit me to interpret this dream.' The Messenger of Allah ﷺ said, "Interpret it." Abū Bakr said, 'As for the cloud, it is the cloud of Islam. As for the dripping butter and honey, that is the Qur'ān; its sweetness and softness. As for the people who are scooping it with their palms, they are those who are benefiting a lot, or little, from the Qur'ān. As for the rope coming down from heaven to earth, it is the truth on which you are on. You hold it and Allah ascends you. After you, another person will hold it and he will ascend. After him, another person will hold it and he will ascend. Another person will hold it and it will break off and it will then be joined for him and he will ascend.'

'O Messenger of Allah! May my father be your protection, tell me am I right or wrong?' The Messenger of Allah ﷺ replied, "You got some right and missed some." Abū Bakr said, 'Then by Allah, O Messenger of Allah, you shall tell me what I said wrong.' The Prophet ﷺ replied, "Do not swear by Allah O Abū Bakr."

Imām Nawawī, in his Commentary[147], said that scholars varied in their interpretations of "You got some right and missed some." Ibn Qutayba and others said, it meant your interpretation is correct but it was wrong to volunteer to interpret it. Other scholars said this opinion is wrong, for the Prophet ﷺ asked Abū Bakr ؓ to interpret the dream. What was missing, they said, was that Abū Bakr ؓ did not interpret it completely. For example, the person saw a cloud dripping butter and honey, Abū Bakr ؓ interpreted this as the sweetness and softness of the Qur'ān, but that applies to honey only. He did not interpret butter which is to be construed as the Sunnah.

Other scholars said that what was missing is interpreting properly the last person who held on to the rope that will break off. This clearly, they said, refers to ʿUthmān ؓ and his voluntary resignation from the Caliphate while Abū Bakr ؓ interpreted that someone else will join the rope for him after it broke off and he will then ascend. The scholars contended that ʿUthmān ؓ was forcefully removed from the Caliphate and murdered with someone else taking his position. The correct interpretation would be that the joining of the rope meant someone else from his clan will reassume his position.

Ibn Ḥajar, in his Commentary on Bukhārī, listed some of what could be learned from this ḥadīth. It is allowed, he said, for a scholar to display his scholarly expertise provided his intentions are pure and free of pretensions.

A scholar may talk about a topic in the presence of a more knowledgeable scholar if he approved that explicitly or implicitly.

The same rule could be applied to issuing edicts or judgments in the presence of a more learned scholar.

A student may oblige his teacher, with an oath, to benefit him with his knowledge. Sometimes a person obliges another by asking him by Allah to comply with his request. The ḥadīth indicates that complying with such an oath is recommended when it does not entail any disadvantage or difficulty, since here the Prophet ﷺ did not comply with Abū Bakr's ؓ request.

On other occasions, the Prophet ﷺ would train his companions by ordering them to rule in his presence on disputes that were brought to him to judge.

❖ ḤADĪTH 91: Imām Aḥmad in his *Musnad* and Dārqutnī in his *Sunan* reported[148] on the authority of ʿAbdullah ibn ʿAmr ibn al-ʿĀṣ (may Allah be pleased with both of them) who said, 'Two men came to the Messenger of Allah ﷺ in a dispute and the Messenger of Allah ﷺ said to ʿAmr ibn al-ʿĀṣ, "You judge between these two." ʿAmr said, 'In your presence O Messenger of Allah?' "Yes." The Prophet replied. ʿAmr asked, 'On what basis should I judge?' The Prophet said, "If you did your best and you judged rightly, you will be rewarded ten-folds. And if you did your best and judged wrongly, you will receive one reward."

This ḥadīth is somewhat odd in the sense that it mentions a tenfold reward, while the more correct version tells of a double reward for those doing their best and judging correctly and one reward if they did their best and judged wrongly.

❖ ḤADĪTH 92: Imām Aḥmad and Dārqutnī reported[149] also on the authority of ʿUqba ibn ʿĀmir al-Juhanī ﷺ who said, 'Two litigants came to the Messenger of Allah ﷺ to settle their dispute. He said to me, "O ʿUqba! Go and judge between them." I said, 'O Messenger of Allah! You deserve that more than me.' He replied, "Even so. Go and judge between them; if you did your best and judged rightly, you will be rewarded ten-fold. And if you you did your best and judged wrongly, you will receive one reward."'

❖ ḤADĪTH 93: Ibn Mājah and Dārqutnī (the text is his) reported[150] on the authority of Jāriya ibn Ẓafar al-Ḥanafī al-Yamāmī ﷺ who said, 'Two brothers who shared a house raised a log partition in its midth. Both passed away leaving behind some children.

Each side claimed the partition belonged exclusively to him and not to the other side. The children of these two brothers asked the Prophet ﷺ to judge and he sent Ḥudhaifa ibn al-Yamān to judge the case. He ruled that the partition belonged to whom he has rope ties on his side. Ḥudhaifa then returned and informed the Prophet ﷺ and the Prophet ﷺ responded, "You got it right and you have done well."

Asking a learner and praising him if he is correct

At times, the Prophet ﷺ used to test some of his companions by asking him a particular question to gauge his aptitude and knowledge. If he answered correctly the Prophet ﷺ would praise him, applaud him and tap him on his chest – pointing out that he has merited the Prophet's ﷺ affection and appreciation because of his right answer.

❖ ḤADĪTH 93: Muslim reported[151] on the authority of Ubayy ibn Kaᶜb ﷺ, whose nickname was Abū al-Mundhir, who said, 'The Messenger of Allah ﷺ said, "O Abū al-Mundhir! Which is the greatest verse of Allah's Book that you have memorised?" I replied, 'Allah and His messenger know best.' He said, 'O Abū al-Mundhir! Do you know which is the greatest verse of Allah's Book that you have memorised?" I replied, 'Allah - there is none worthy of worship but He. The Ever-Living, the Sustaining'[152] he said, 'The Prophet then patted me on my chest and said, "Congratulations on your knowledge O Abū al-Mundhir."'

❖ ḤADĪTH 95: Abū Dāwūd, Tirmidhī, Dārimī, Ibn Saᶜd and Qāḍī Wakīᶜ reported[153] on the authority of Muᶜādh ibn Jabal ﷺ who said, 'when the Messenger of Allah ﷺ posted me to Yemen, he asked me, "How will you judge if a judgement was referred to you?" I replied, 'I will judge by the Qur'ān.' He asked, "What if you did not find it in Allah's Book?" I replied, 'I will judge by the Sunnah of the Messenger of Allah.' He asked, "And if you did not find it in the Sunnah of the Messenger of Allah?" I replied, "I will use my own judgment to the best of my ability.' The Messenger of Allah patted my chest with his hand and said, "All praise be to Allah who guided the envoy of the Messenger of Allah to what pleases the Messenger of Allah."'

Teaching by tacit approval

This is one of the categories of the Sunnah. Scholars of jurisprudence and ḥadīth refer to it as *taqrīr* or approval. This is defined as the act or the saying of a Muslim in the presence of the Prophet ﷺ who noticed it and kept silent or condoned it. This is a tacit approval by the Prophet ﷺ of that particular act or saying. Many scholarly issues were learnt from the Prophet ﷺ in this way. I will cite just two ḥadīths as examples.

❖ ḤADĪTH 96: Bukhārī reported on the authority of Abū Juḥaifa Wahb ibn ʿAbdullah ؓ who said, "The Prophet ﷺ declared Salmān and Abū Dardā' brothers. One time, Salmān visited Abū Dardā' and he noticed that, his brother's wife, Umm al-Dardā', was wearing shabby clothes. Salmān asked her, 'What's wrong?' She replied, 'Your brother Abū Dardā' is not interested in worldly life.'

When Abū Dardā' came he prepared some food and invited Salmān and he said to Salmān, 'You eat, because I am fasting,' Salmān replied, 'I will not eat unless you also eat.' So he also ate. At night, Abū Dardā' went to pray and Salmān said to him, 'Sleep!' So he slept and woke up later to pray and again Salmān told him, 'Sleep!' When the end of the night approached, Salmān said to him,

'You may get up now.' The two of them then prayed. Salmān then said to him, 'Indeed your Lord has a right over you, your body has a right over you and your family has a right over you. Give each his due right.'

Abū Dardā' then went to the Prophet ﷺ and told him the full story and the Prophet ﷺ commented, "Salmān was spoke correctly."'

That the Prophet ﷺ fully endorsed what Salmān said and did, is an indication of the high quality of Salmān. The Prophet ﷺ added, according to the narration of Ibn Saᶜd, that, "Salmān is filled with knowledge."

It is worth mentioning that the Prophet ﷺ twice declared a full brotherhood bond between certain companions. Ibn Ḥajar, in his Commentary, said the Prophet's biographers mentioned that he twice declared brotherhood. The first, before Hijra, was among Muhājirīn to support and console each other, such as the brotherhood of Zaid ibn Ḥāritha and Ḥamza ibn ᶜAbdul Muṭṭalib. The second, after Hijra, was between Anṣār and Muhājirīn, such as the brotherhood of ᶜAbdur Raḥmān ibn ᶜAwf and Saᶜd ibn ar-Rabīᶜ.

The narration of Tirmidhī added, 'and your guest has a right over you.' Dārqutnī's narration concluded with a more elaborated advice, 'So fast and break fast. Pray at night and sleep. And enjoy your wife.'

❖ ḤADĪTH 97: Abū Dāwūd reported[154] on the authority of ᶜAmr ibn al-ᶜĀṣ (may Allah be pleased with both of them) who said, 'I had a wet dream on a cold night during the expedition of Dhāt as-Salāsil. I feared that I would die if I took a bath, so I substituted it with dusting my limbs *tayammum* and led my group in the dawn prayer. They mentioned this to the Prophet ﷺ and he asked, "O ᶜAmr! You led your group in prayer while in a state of impurity?" So I told him what prevented me from taking a bath and said,

'I heard Allah saying, "Do not kill yourselves. Allah is certainly Merciful towards you."[155] The Messenger of Allah ﷺ then laughed and said nothing.'

The Prophet's ﷺ smiling is an endorsement of this act of substitution during severe cold weather. This is because the Prophet ﷺ would never approve, even tacitly, anything that is unlawful. In this case, smiling is even a stronger indication of approval than remaining silent.

Teaching whenever an opportunity arises

On many instances, the Prophet ﷺ would seize an appropriate opportunity to drive home a point. He would link the current situation to the knowledge that he wants to disseminate and as such his listeners would fully and clearly understand him.

❖ ḤADĪTH 98: Muslim reported[156] on the authority of Jābir ﷺ who said that, 'The Messenger of Allah ﷺ walked through the market entering it via al-ʿĀlia. People walked with him on both sides and he passed by a dead ewe with tiny ears. He grabbed it by its ears and said, "Which of you would like to buy this for one dirham?" The people replied, 'We would not even want it for free. What would we do with it?' The Prophet said, "Would you like it for free?" The people replied, 'By Allah, had it been alive, the tiny ears would have made it undesirable, let alone when it is dead!' The Prophet ﷺ said, "By Allah, this world is more insignificant in the sight of Allah than this is in your sight."'

❖ ḤADĪTH 99: Bukhārī and Muslim reported[157] on the authority of ʿUmar ibn al-Khaṭṭāb ﷺ who said, 'A group of prisoners of war were brought to the Prophet ﷺ and among them was a woman whose breasts were flowing with milk and she was running around looking for her infant child. When she found her infant, she grabbed him, clung him to her bosom and fed him. Then the Prophet ﷺ said to us, "Do you think that she would throw her child in the fire?" We replied, 'No. As long as she can she will protect him.' The Prophet said, "Indeed Allah is more merciful to His servants than this woman is to her child."'

The Prophet ﷺ seized the opportunity when it presented itself before him and his companions wherein they witnessed the affection of a mother who found her lost child. The Prophet ﷺ compared and likened her mercy to the compassion of Allah in order to teach the companions the kindness of the Creator to His servants. He did not approach the topic of Allah's mercy out of the blue, but he brought it to their attention on this occasion to illustrate for them in a vivid way the infinite mercy of Allah and his kindness toward His servants. As Allah said in the Qur'ān[158], "And Allah is extremely Kind to His servants."

Ibn Ḥajar, in his Commentary, said that among the benefits of this ḥadīth is the Prophet ﷺ 'giving a tangible example of an intangible concept.'

❖ ḤADĪTH **100:** Bukhārī reported on the authority of Jarīr ibn ʿAbdullah al-Bajalī ؓ who said, 'One night while we were sitting with the Prophet ﷺ, he looked at the full moon and said, "On the Day of Resurrection you will see your Lord just as you are seeing this moon without any difficulty. If you can maintain a prayer before sunrise and a prayer before sunset, you should pray it." He then recited the verse[159], "And glorify the praises of your Lord before sunrise and before sunset."'

The Prophet ﷺ took the opportunity of the companions seeing the full moon to explain to them that the believers will be able to see Allah in the hereafter with such clarity and ease.

WISDOM, HUMOUR, & STORIES

The Prophet ﷺ would sometimes joke and jest with his companions, though he spoke nothing but the truth, as he told his companions in the ḥadīth reported by al-Tirmidhī[160] on the authority of Abū Hurayra ؓ, 'The companions said, 'O Messenger of Allah! You joke with us?' "Though I speak nothing but the truth." He replied."

The Prophet ﷺ taught many topics through jokes and humour because gentle humour brings relief and lessens the burdens of difficulties one may come across and live with. Life is never without sourness or troubles and humour lessens its effects on us.

A smile or a grin would teach much more than a stern look or a frown. Occasional humour or an appropriate joke would reinvigorate our minds and spirits while continuous serious teaching will dull our senses and exhaust our thinking. A purposeful humour would bring us back more ready and attentive. All of which show us how the Prophet ﷺ was a wise teacher and a kind educator.

Ibn Qutayba elaborated on this[161], 'The Prophet ﷺ would joke because people are commanded to emulate him and to follow his guidance. Had he forsaken smiles and pleasantness and remained serious and stern all of his time, people would feel obliged to follow suit, though this would be difficult as it is against human nature and instincts. The Prophet ﷺ joked so that they may joke, but he spoke nothing but the truth.'

Imām Nawawī in his *Adhkār*[162] said, 'Joking is prohibited when it becomes excessive and incessant for it leads to triviality and recklessness. It diverts away from the remembrance of Allah and from paying attention to religious duties. On many occasions, it causes harm and leads to ill will, resentment and disrespect. But jokes and humour that are free from all this could be practiced as the Prophet ﷺ used to do from time to time, when appropriate, to please his companions and to bring them closer to him.

❖ ḤADĪTH **101:** Bukhārī, Muslim, Tirmidhī, Ibn Mājah and Abū Dāwūd (the text is his) reported[163] on the authority of Anas ibn Mālik ﷺ who said, 'The Messenger of Allah ﷺ used to visit us frequently. I had a younger brother nick-named Abū ʿUmayr who had a red-beaked bird with which he used to play. This bird died and when the Prophet came to visit us, he saw that my brother was sad and he asked, "What is wrong with him?" They said, 'His bird has died.' The Prophet, said to him, "O Abū ʿUmayr! What did your birdie do?"'

There are many rules and lessons that could be drawn from this ḥadīth, among them:

The leader may favour some of his followers with a visit.

The leader can socialise with certain followers without doing the same to others.

A scholar may take the initiative and teach the learners as opposed to them seeking it.

Joking is allowed including that with an immature child.

We can give a person who has no children a nick name based on possibly the name of his child.

Children may play with birds as pets as long as they do not

harm them. Parents or guardians may allow them to do so.

We may spend money on acceptable amusements for children.

The tolerability of keeping birds in cages and other enclosures.

Dealing with people according to their intellects and understanding.

We may address a person by his diminutive name, as long as we are causing no offence, as the Prophet ﷺ addressed the young child by "Abū ʿUmayr" which is the diminutive form of ʿUmar.

We are allowed to ask a question though we may know the answer as long as we intend no mockery. The Prophet ﷺ asked, "What did your birdie do?" despite knowing that it had died.

It is interesting to note that some scholars devoted a full chapter to comment on this brief ḥadīth as Imām Ibn Ḥajar in *Fatḥ al-Bārī* and to bring sixty lessons and rules. My teacher ʿAbdul Ḥayy al-Kittānī mentioned that other scholars came out with three hundred lessons. The historian of Maghrib and Andalusia, al-Maqqarī, in his book *Nafiḥ aṭ-Ṭīb* mentioned that the scholar Ibn aṣ-Ṣabbāgh, in his lesson in Meknes dictated five hundred lessons and rules just from this ḥadīth.

❖ ḤADĪTH **102:** Abū Dāwūd and Tirmidhī reported[164] on the authority of Anas ﷺ that, 'A man asked the Messenger of Allah ﷺ to give him a ride (i.e. a camel). The Messenger of Allah ﷺ said to him, "I'll give you the child of a camel." The man said, 'O Messenger of Allah! What can I do with the child of a camel?' Then the Messenger of Allah ﷺ replied, "Are not all camels children of camels?"'

Through this quick and subtle wit, the Prophet ﷺ taught the man that a camel, even when old enough to carry loads, is still the child of a camel.

The Prophet ﷺ, in this ḥadīth, drew the attention of the learners and others to reflect over what they had heard and not to refute it right away. A very important manner the student should enjoy if he is to succeed.

Another lesson we draw is that the Teacher Prophet may joke while saying nothing but the truth.

Another lesson is to pay attention to minute details of what we hear or learn.

Emphasizing a topic with an oath

Frequently, the Prophet ﷺ would commence his speech by taking an oath in the name of Allah. This was to draw attention to the importance of what he was about to say, to reinforce it and to emphasise it.

Ibn al-Qayyim said[165], 'The Prophet ﷺ took an oath on more than 80 occasions as reported in the books of ḥadīth. Allah commanded him, in three instances in the Qur'ān, to take an oath over what he was saying, "Say: Yes! By my Sustainer! It is verily the truth!" "Say: Yes! By my Sustainer! It will come to you." "Say: Yes! By my Sustainer! You will certainly be resurrected."'[166]

❖ ḤADĪTH **103:** Muslim[167] reported on the authority of Abū Hurayra ؓ who said, 'The Messenger of Allah ﷺ said, "By Him who has my soul in His hand, you will not enter paradise until you believe and you will not believe until you love each other. Shall I guide you to what you may do so you will love each other? Spread greetings of peace amongst you."'

Imām Nawawī said in his Commentary, 'This ḥadīth includes a great encouragement to spread greetings among all Muslims - those whom one knows and those whom one does not know. A greeting with peace and blessings is the first step of friendliness and the key to bringing affection. By spreading it, Muslims establish a strong bond among themselves and, at the same time, display their distinct motto. To initiate greetings is an exercise in humbleness so it may become a personal trait. It is also a show of respect to other Muslims. Judge 'Iyāḍ said that 'friendliness is one of the duties of the faith, a pillar of *Sharīʿa* and a common theme in Islam.''

The ḥadīth and those following it implies that, based on the Prophet's oath, one, whether a teacher or not, can take an oath without being asked to do so in order to show the importance of what he is saying or to stress its authenticity, attributes and effects.

❖ ḤADĪTH **104:** Muslim reported[168] on the authority of Anas ﷺ that 'the Prophet ﷺ said, "By Him who has my soul in His hand, a person doesn't believe unless he loves for his neighbour - or he said for his brother - what he loves for himself."'

The scholars said that "brother" here refers to brotherhood among humans which combines non-Muslims and Muslims. Thus, a person should like for his non-Muslim brother what he likes for himself such as being a Muslim. Likewise, he should like for his Muslim brother to remain a practicing Muslim. As such, Islam recommends praying for the guidance of non-Muslims.

That the Prophet ﷺ said "he doesn't believe" is understood to mean "he doesn't enjoy solid faith."

❖ ḤADĪTH **105:** Bukhārī[169] reported on the authority of Abū Shuraiḥ al-Khuzāʿī ﷺ that 'the Messenger of Allah ﷺ said, "By Allah, he does not believe! By Allah, he does not believe! By Allah, he does not believe!" He was asked, 'Who? O Messenger of Allah!' "A person whose neighbour feels unsafe of his mischief." He answered.

The Prophet ﷺ made an oath in each of the above ḥadīths. As he was fully trusted and never lied, this was exclusively to highlight the importance of greeting in reinforcing friendship and affection amongst the people, to draw attention to the importance of desiring good for neighbours and brothers and to draw attention to the repugnance of causing harm or disturbance to neighbours. Also, the Prophet ﷺ stressed how important these manners are by describing, as incomplete believers, those who do not practise them.

Repeating words three times for emphasise

The Prophet ﷺ would repeat his words in order to emphasise the topic, to draw the attention of those listening to its importance and to enable listeners to fully comprehend it beyond doubt. Highlighting this, Imām Bukhārī titled a chapter in his *Ṣaḥīḥ*[170] 'Chapter on repeating a speech three times so that it is understood.' In that chapter he reported the next two ḥadīths.

Ibn Ḥajar, in his Commentary[171], quoted Ibn al-Munayyir, 'Through this chapter, Bukhārī dismissed the argument of those who disliked the repetition of a ḥadīth and who considered such a request to be a sign of dumbness.' He adds, 'But in fact this differs according to aptitudes and if a student cannot memorise from the first time, it is completely perfect for him to ask for it to be repeated. The teacher has no excuse for not obliging. In fact, repetition becomes more incumbent upon the teacher to conclude what he has commenced. Ibn at-Tīn said the ḥadīth indicates that teachers fulfil their duties with three repetitions."

Also, Bukhārī titled another chapter[172] 'On hearing what he couldn't understand and asking for clarification to understand it.' In this chapter, he reported the ḥadīth of Ibn Abī Mulaika that ʿĀ'isha, the wife of the Prophet ﷺ, used to question anything she did not comprehend till it was clarified. Once the Prophet ﷺ said, "Whoever is questioned [on the Day of Judgement] will be punished." ʿĀ'isha said, 'I asked, doesn't Allah say "He will have an easy account." She continued, the Prophet ﷺ said, "That is the review – Whoever is questioned will be punished."'

Ibn Ḥajar, in his Commentary[173], said this ḥadīth shows how keen ʿĀ'isha was to learn the meaning of a ḥadīth. It shows that the Prophet ﷺ was never angry with questions of knowledge. It indicates we are allowed to debate and to compare ḥadīth with Qur'ān.

❖ ḤADĪTH **106:** Bukhārī reported[174] on the authority of Anas ؓ, 'that when the Prophet ﷺ gave a speech he would repeat it three times so that it is well understood by his listeners.'

❖ ḤADĪTH **107:** Bukhārī reported[175] on the authority of ʿAbdullah ibn ʿAmr (may Allah be pleased with both of them) who said, 'The Messenger of Allah ﷺ arrived delayed on one journey. He caught up with us just before *ʿAṣr* afternoon prayer was about to expire and we were performing ablution and wiping our feet. The Prophet called out, twice or three times, in his loudest voice, "Save your heels from the hellfire."'

Here the Prophet ﷺ warned those who do not wash their feet thoroughly during ablution. This ḥadīth indicates that teaching an ignorant person is mandatory, the voice can be raised when rebuking someone and an issue can be repeated to make it thoroughly understood.

Ibn Ḥajar, in his Commentary, said 'two or three' came in this ḥadīth because the narrator was not quite sure. But that indicates that repeating three times is not a must. The goal is to understand and once it is achieved, one can stop.

❖ ḤADĪTH **108:** Imām Aḥmad reported in his Musnad[176] on the authority of ʿAbdur Raḥmān ibn Ghanm on the authority of Muʿādh ibn Jabal ؓ that the Messenger of Allah ﷺ set out with his people towards the battle of Tabūk. At dawn, he led the Fajr prayer and then people rode their camels but they began dozing off once the sun rose as they have travelled during the night. Muʿādh kept with the Messenger of Allah ﷺ following his tracks. Then the Messenger of Allah ﷺ lifted his veil around his head and looked back. He saw that Muʿādh was the nearest man to him from the army. The Messenger of Allah ﷺ called out to him, "O Muʿādh!" He replied, 'Here I am, O Prophet of Allah!' He said, "Come close." So he went close to him till their camels touched. Then the Messenger of Allah ﷺ said, "I did not realise people were so far behind." Muʿādh replied, 'O Prophet of Allah! People became sleepy and the animals divided and moved on their own - grazing and roaming.' The the Messenger of Allah ﷺ said, "I was also sleepy."

When Muʿādh ؓ saw the Messenger of Allah's ﷺ relaxation and alone with him, he said, 'O Messenger of Allah! Allow me to ask you a question that has troubled me and caused me sickness and depression.' The Prophet of Allah ﷺ replied, "Ask whatever you want."

He said, 'O Prophet of Allah! Inform me of a deed that will admit me into paradise. I have no other question beside it.' The Prophet of Allah ﷺ replied, "Excellent! Excellent! Excellent! You have asked about a very serious matter. You have asked about a very serious matter. You have asked about a very serious matter. And it is extremely easy for whom Allah blessed with goodness. It is extremely easy for whom Allah blessed with goodness. It is extremely easy for whom Allah blessed with goodness." Everything that the Prophet told him, he said it three times so that he would fully comprehend it. Then the Prophet of Allah ﷺ said, "You must believe in Allah and in the Last Day, establish prayers, worship Allah alone - without ascribing anything to Him. You continue with all this till you die." Muʿādh said, 'O Prophet of Allah! Repeat it to me.' So he repeated it to him three times.

The Prophet of Allah ﷺ, then said, "O Muʿādh! If you wish, I will tell you the main principle of this religion, the foundation of this religion and the culmination of this religion." Muʿādh said, 'May my parents protect you O Prophet of Allah! You should certainly tell me.' The Prophet of Allah ﷺ then said, "The principle of this religion is to testify that there is none worthy of worship but Allah, He is one and has no partner and Muḥammad is His servant and messenger. The body of this religion is praying regularly and paying Zakat. The culmination of this religion is Jihād in the cause of Allah. I have been commanded to fight the people until they establish the prayers, pay Zakat, testify that there is none worthy of worship but Allah, He is one and has no partner and that Muḥammad is His servant and messenger. If they do that, then they have protected their blood and wealth, except according to law. Their reckoning is with Allah, Mighty and Majestic is He..."'

Emphasis by changing postures or repeating

At times the Prophet ﷺ would change his posture and manner while repeating what he had just said to convey the importance and gravity of what he was saying or warning against.

❖ ḤADĪTH **109:** Bukhārī (the text is his) and Muslim reported on the authority of Abū Bakra ؓ who said, 'that the Messenger of Allah ﷺ said, "Shall I not inform you of the greatest of sins? Shall I not inform you of the greatest of sins? Shall I not inform you of the greatest of sins?" We said, 'Certainly O Messenger of Allah' He said, "Ascribing partners to Allah and disobeying parents." At the time he was reclining, but then he sat up and then said, "And surely false statement and false witness. And surely false statement and false witness." He continued to repeat that until I said to myself, 'He is never going to stop.' And in the narration of Muslim, 'He continued to repeat that till we said, 'If only he would stop.'"

The Prophet ﷺ repeated his questions in the beginning to prepare the listeners to what he is going to say so they may pay full attention.

The Prophet ﷺ repeated his words and changed his posture to draw attention to the gravity of the false testimony that he was warning against.

Though the Prophet ﷺ here warned against ascribing partners to Allah, the warning applies to the worst forms such as atheism. The Prophet ﷺ stressed idolatry since it was very common among the tribes of Arabia.

Shaikh Abū ʿAmr ibn aṣ-Ṣalāḥ in his Edicts defined disobedience of parents as 'every act that causes extraordinary displeasure to the father or the mother, provided it is not a obligatory act. Or perhaps it could be redefined as: Obeying parents is mandatory as long as it does not concern a disobedient ḥarām act.'

The words "false statement" and "false witness" mean basically the same. They were brought together for broadening the meaning and emphasizing it.

We may notice that the Prophet ﷺ repeated "a false statement and a false witness" and did not repeat "Ascribing partners to Allah and disobedience to parents." This was to demonstrate how keen he was to forewarn against false testimony, because people commit this sin more easily and are care less about it so its harm is more frequent. Ascribing partners to Allah is repugnant to Muslims. Disobedience to parents is repugnant to human nature. But when it comes to false testimony, there are many reasons and motives that may cause it and the Prophet ﷺ, appropriately, focused on it for this reason not because it is more serious than ascribing partners or disbelief in Allah for these are the worst of sins.

False witness is to lie in a statement to attain a wrong result such as destroying lives, gaining wealth, or devouring the rights of other people. None of the major sins, excluding *shirk* are more harmful and disruptive. As such it was equated to ascribing partners to Allah and the Prophet ﷺ warned against it so strongly and repeatedly in a manner that he did not apply to other crimes such as murder and fornication.

Ibn Ḥajar, in his Commentary[177], said, 'We learn from this ḥadīth the desirability of repeating a reminder three times so that it is fully understood. The person giving the reminder may display his apprehension so that its implications and undesirability are fully realised. Also, a student should be concerned about his teacher if he sees him agitated and he should wish him to calm down and return to his normal mood.'

The ḥadīth indicates that a speaker may prepare his audience and may ask them to pay full attention to what he is going to tell them.

Drawing attention by repeating a call and delaying the answer

On certain occasions, the Prophet ﷺ would call a person a few times without engaging him. This is to generate curiosity and attention to what the Prophet ﷺ was going to say and so that his listeners would focus exclusively on that.

❖ ḤADĪTH **110:** Muslim and Bukhārī (the text is his) reported[178] on the authority of Muʿādh ibn Jabal ؓ who said, 'Whilst I was riding behind the Prophet ﷺ, there was nothing between me and him except the wood end of the saddle when he said, "O Muʿādh!" I replied, 'Here I am O Messenger of Allah, fully at your disposal.' He kept silent for an hour then said, "O Muʿādh!" I replied, 'Here I am O Messenger of Allah, fully at your disposal.' He kept silent for another hour then said, "O Muʿādh ibn Jabal!" I replied, 'Here I am O Messenger of Allah, fully at your disposal.' He said, "Do you know what right Allah has over His servants?" I replied, 'Allah and His Messenger know best.' He said, "The right of Allah over His servants is that they worship Him without ascribing any partner to Him."

He kept silent for another hour and then said, "O Muʿādh ibn Jabal!" I replied, 'Here I am O Messenger of Allah! At your disposal.' He said, "Do you know the right of the servants with Allah if they fulfilled that?" I replied, 'Allah and His messenger know best.' He said, "The right of servants with Allah is that He will not penalise them." Muʿādh described how close he was to the Prophet ﷺ in order to illustrate how vividly he remembers what he heard from him. The Prophet ﷺ in this instance was riding a donkey as the narration of Muslim reveals.

The Prophet ﷺ repeatedly called Muʿādh, while deliberately saying nothing, to emphasise the importance of what he was about to say and to have the full attention of Muʿādh to what he was about to hear, so that he may understand and ponder it.

Some scholars mentioned that "the right of servants with Allah" is not identical to "the right of Allah upon His servants." The use of the word "right" is for figurative comparison.

Ibn Ḥajar, in his Commentary, listed the following educational themes that could be learnt from this ḥadīth: The politeness of Muʿādh when conversing with the Prophet ﷺ and referring what he does not know to the Prophet ﷺ; Muʿādh was close and dear to the Prophet ﷺ; repeating sentences to emphasise their context and ensure they are fully understood; the teacher may ask his student to test the latter's knowledge and to explain to him what he may not understand.

Holding the hand or shoulder of the listener to attain his interest

At times the Prophet ﷺ would hold the hand or shoulder of his listener to attain his interest and get his full attention to what he is teaching him, so that he may focus all his senses to it and as such will never forget it.

❖ ḤADĪTH **111:** Muslim and Bukhārī (the text is his) reported[179] on the authority of ʿAbdullah ibn Sakhra Abī Maʿmar who said, 'I heard Ibn Masʿūd say, 'The Messenger of Allah ﷺ taught me, while my palm was between his palms, the Prayers of Greetings *Tashahhud* just as he would teach me a chapter from the Qur'ān.'

The ḥadīth shows us how keen the Prophet ﷺ was on teaching the Prayers of Greetings *Tashahhud.*

The teacher must show how interested he is in teaching his students an important issue and to draw their attention to its importance so that they may pay full attention to him. With such attention and awareness they will fully remember his words, actions, gestures and expressions without any additions, omission, changes, substitutions or carelessness

Teaching and instructing under conditions that will act as a reminder to the student, e.g. being very close to the student and holding his hand so that he is more attentive and fully aware of what he is being taught compared to teaching in a common and ordinary manner.

The teacher may give extra attention to certain students because of their intelligence, promising future, or perceiving judiciousness and originality in them.

❖ ḤADĪTH **112:** Bukhārī and Tirmidhī reported on the authority of ʿAbdullah ibn ʿUmar (may Allah be pleased with both of them) who said, 'The Messenger of Allah ﷺ held me by my shoulder and said, "Be in this world as though you are a stranger or a traveller, and consider yourself amongst those in the graves."

Ibn ʿUmar, the narrator of this ḥadīth, used to say 'When you come to the evening, don't expect to live in the morning. And when you wake up in the morning don't expect to live to the evening. Keep some of health for times of sickness and some of your life for your death, for you never know whether you will be called 'the deceased' tomorrow.'

You should consider yourself among those in the graves because you are certainly going to die as death is part of your physiology and life. ʿUmar ibn ʿAbdul ʿAzīz said, 'A person who is not separated from his father Adam by a living being is deeply rooted in death.' Day after day, you see people, relatives and strangers, die, so you will one day. ʿUmar ibn al-Khaṭṭāb used to say, 'Every day we hear that so and so has died and eventually one day someone will say, ʿUmar has died.' A poet has said, 'We live and die every day and night. A day will come that we will not survive.'

The Prophet ﷺ gradually reminded ʿAbdullah ibn ʿUmar. First, he drew the example of the stranger, the passer-by and then those who reached their graves. A stranger moves, in his journey, from one place to another while his mind is fixed on concluding his journey. He does not burden himself by carrying too many possessions and he remains in a place only as long as he must or needs.

As for the passer-by, his main concern is to reach his destination. He therefore does not pay attention to distractions and he is unlikely to stop to marvel over a beautiful garden, a breezy spot, or a nice shade.

Those in their graves are preceding us to meeting Allah. Those alive will tread the path sooner or later.

Ibn Ḥajar, in his Commentary, listed a few points we can learn from this ḥadīth. A teacher during instructions or a lecturer during a sermon may touch their listeners to put them at ease and to make them more interested. Usually, this is only done with those inclined to that. Sometimes the Prophet ﷺ address or advice to one person is applicable to all.

The Prophet's ﷺ dedication to bring goodness to his people.

The advice not to indulge in the pleasures of this world and to take only what is necessary. For the same purpose, the Prophet ﷺ would occasionally lightly pat the thigh of a companion, as was the habit of the Arabs of the time.

❖ ḤADĪTH **113:** Muslim reported[180] that the senior follower of the companions *Tābi'ī*, Abū al-ʿĀliya said, 'The Amīr, Ibn Ziyād, delayed the prayers. When ʿAbdullah ibn aṣ-Ṣāmit came to me. I offered him a chair on which he sat and then told him what Ibn Ziyād did. He bit onto his lip and patted my thigh and said, 'I asked Abū Dharr your question and he patted my thigh, just as I have patted your thigh and said, 'I had asked the Messenger of Allah ﷺ the same question and he patted my thigh, just as I have patted your thigh and said, "Offer your prayers on time. If a group is to pray, pray with them and do not say, 'I'm not going to pray since I have already prayed - This prayer is additional good."''

Imām Nawawī, in his Commentary on Muslim, said that the Prophet ﷺ patted the thigh of the companion to draw his attention and to focus his thoughts on what he was saying.

Saying little to prompt further inquiry

At times the Prophet ﷺ would be a little ambiguous to prompt his listener to inquire more about what he has just heard. This, in turn, would make the talk more memorable and the listener more keen on applying it.

❖ ḤADĪTH **114:** Imām Aḥmad reported[181] on the authority of Anas ibn Mālik ﷺ who said, 'While we were sitting with the Messenger of Allah ﷺ he said, "Soon a man from the people of paradise will join you." Soon thereafter, a man from the Anṣār appeared - his beard dripping from ablution and holding his sandals with his left hand. The next day, the Prophet ﷺ said the same thing and the same person appeared in the same manner. On the third day, the Prophet ﷺ said the same thing again and the same person appeared in the same manner.'

'When the Prophet ﷺ left, ʿAbdullah ibn ʿAmr followed that man and said to him, 'I had an argument with my father and I swore not to enter his home for three days. Would you be kind to accommodate me for these three days?' The man replied, 'Yes."

Anas said, "ʿAbdullah used to say that he remained with him for three nights but did not see that man getting up to pray at night except that when he would toss and turn on his bed, he would praise Allah, Mighty and Majestic is He and glorify Him till he eventually got up for the dawn prayer.'

ʿAbdullah said, 'However, I never heard him say anything but good. When these three days passed and I was almost belittling his deeds, I asked him, 'O servant of Allah! There was no argument or dispute between me and my father. In fact, I heard the Messenger of Allah ﷺ saying three times, "Soon a man from the people of paradise will join you," and each time you appeared. I therefore wanted to stay with you and see what you do, so that I could follow your example. But I did not see you doing much, so how did you attain the rank the Messenger of Allah ﷺ mentioned?' The man replied, 'All I do is what you have seen.' When I left, he called me and said, 'O my nephew! All I do is what you have seen but in addition

I bear no deceit to any Muslim and I do not envy anyone for the good which Allah has given him.' ʿAbdullah said, 'This is what elevated you and this is what we cannot carry on."

The man referred to in this ḥadīth is Saʿd ibn Abī Waqqāṣ as revealed by other narrators and historians.

It is the tradition of the Prophet ﷺ to hold shoes in the left hand.

The ḥadīth highlights the high standing of Saʿd ibn Abī Waqqāṣ to the extent that the Prophet ﷺ named him among the people of paradise. As such, he is one of the ten who were assured of entering paradise.

One should follow the example of ʿAbdullah ibn ʿAmr in his keen desire to follow the example of the righteous and the pious in their good deeds.

The Prophet ﷺ encouraged his followers to do good by praising those who do good without specifying the reasons, leaving that to his listeners to find out. This will leave a deeper impression on them.

The ḥadīth highlights the virtue of purifying and cleansing the heart from deceit and envy. Such attitude may qualify us for paradise.

ʿAbdullah ibn ʿAmr claimed that he had an argument with his father to be able to stay with the virtuous companion and witness what he does to merit such a distinction. This scheme is acceptable from an Islamic perspective as it does not contravene the objectives of the *Sharīʿa*. The crucial criterion in an accepted scheme is that it aims to reclaim a right, to fend off an injustice, to perform a duty, to hinder an illegitimate act, to attain a right, to reveal a wrong, or to obtain a legitimate favour, etc... All these, or similar, legitimate objectives must be achieved without infringing upon the rights of the Creator or His creatures[182].

Outlining the issue then giving its details

Occasionally, the Prophet ﷺ will list the outlines of an issue to raise interest in his listeners to ask further and investigate it more. Later, the Prophet ﷺ would explain it in clear details making the issue more memorable and understandable to his listeners.

❖ ḤADĪTH **115:** Bukhārī, Muslim (the text is his) and Ibn Mājah reported[183] on the authority of Anas ibn Mālik ﷺ who said, 'A funeral passed by and the deceased was praised upon which the Prophet of Allah ﷺ said, "It's due. It's due. It's due." Another funeral passed by and the deceased was condemned upon which the Prophet of Allah ﷺ said, "It's due. It's due. It's due."

ʿUmar said, 'May my parents protect you. A funeral proceeded and the deceased was praised and you said, "It's due. It's due. It's due." Another funeral passed by and the deceased was condemned and you said, "It's due. It's due. It's due." Then the Messenger of Allah ﷺ said, "Whomever you praise deserves paradise. And whomever you spoke evil of deserves hell. You are the witnesses of Allah on earth. You are the witnesses of Allah on earth. You are the witnesses of Allah on earth."'

The Prophet ﷺ told his companions that they are "the witnesses of Allah on earth," but the scholars explained that this virtue extends beyond the companions to all who follow them among the righteous and believers.

Some scholars said that this ḥadīth means that if virtuous and righteous people praised and spoke good of a person and he was truly good, then he will among the people of paradise. However, if he was not truly good such a praise will not take him to paradise.

Other scholars said that if a Muslim passed away and people were inspired to praise him, then this is an indication that he is among the people of paradise, irrespective of whether his deeds deserve that or not- this is completely subservient to the will of Allah who may forgive whoever he wills.

The ḥadīth encourages emphasising important issues by repeating it a few times to ensure it is memorised and understood and will be practiced by those who heard it.

The ḥadīth encourages us to outline an issue before going into its details. This way we prepare the listener with an overview so he becomes more eager to listen to the details and to place it in the general perspectives.

❖ ḤADĪTH **116:** Muslim reported[184] on the authority of Maᶜbad ibn Kaᶜb ibn Mālik on the authority of Qatāda ibn Ribᶜī ﷺ who used to narrate that, 'a funeral passed by and the Messenger of Allah ﷺ said, "One is enjoying relief and another is leaving relief behind him." They said, 'O Messenger of Allah! Who is which?' He said, "A believing servant is relieved from the exhaustion of this world to the mercy of Allah and a wrong-acting servant is the one from whom people, lands, trees and animals are relieved."

Imām Nawawī, in his Commentary on Muslim, said the ḥadīth indicates that the dead are of two types - those who attain relief and those whose death brings relief to others. The death of a mischievous person brings relief to people whom he may have brought harm to. Harm to humans could take many forms such as injustice, oppression and perpetrating evils. If they denounced it they will face dire consequences and if they remained silent, they will be committing a sin also.

The death of such a person will bring relief to the animals that he used to hurt, beat, overload, under-feed and other similar forms of abuse. Lands and trees will obtain relief because, it is said, his sins may prevent rain, or because he may unjustly confiscate it, abuse it, or divert its water to his own use.

Another ḥadīth showing the Prophet ﷺ using this style is the ḥadīth warning against harming neighbours:

❖ ḤADĪTH **117:** Bukhārī reported[185] on the authority of Abū Shuraiḥ al-Khuzāʿī ﷺ that 'the Messenger of Allah ﷺ said, "By Allah, he does not believe! By Allah, he does not believe! By Allah, he does not believe!" He was asked, 'Who, O Messenger of Allah?' "A person whose neighbour feels unsafe of his mischief." He answered.

A fourth ḥadīth in which the Prophet ﷺ used this style, is the ḥadīth warning against mistreating parents:

❖ ḤADĪTH **118:** Muslim reported[186] on the authority of Abū Hurayra ﷺ who said, 'The Messenger of Allah ﷺ said, "May his nose be rubbed in dust, may his nose be rubbed in dust, may his nose be rubbed in dust!" He was asked, 'Who, O Messenger of Allah?' He said, "Whose parents, both or one, reach old age with him, but he does not enter the Paradise."'

Giving a number then detailing it one by one

A somewhat similar teaching method of the Prophet ﷺ is to say the number of points and then explain them one by one. Numbering items makes it easy to remember without doubts and to fully understand them.

❖ ḤADĪTH **119:** al-Ḥakim reported in *al-Mustadrak*[187] on the authority of Ibn ʿAbbās (may Allah be pleased with both of them) who said, 'The Messenger of Allah ﷺ said, "Take advantage of five before five: your youth before your old age, your good health before your illness, your prosperity before your poverty, your free time before you become too busy and your life before your death."'

This ḥadīth draws our attention to the importance of these five matters and their great benefit. Each of the five are not truly appreciated till they are gone and replaced by its opposite.

❖ ḤADĪTH **120:** Bukhārī and Muslim reported[188] on the authority of Abū Hurayra ﷺ that 'the Prophet ﷺ said, "A wife is married for four reasons: her wealth, her status, her beauty and her religiosity. Get the religious one, may your hands become soiled."

The words "may your hands become soiled" are used to allude to poverty but means the opposite as to say 'follow this or face poverty.'

Imām Nawawī, in his Commentary[189], said the ḥadīth urges us to seek the company of religious people at all times. Being in their company, a person will benefit from their manners, blessings and noble behaviour. At the same time, he can be sure they will not harm him.

Cautioning and reminding

Cautioning and reminding were among the most important and most prominent methods the Prophet ﷺ used in his teaching. This is a reflection of the orders of the Qur'ān wherein Allah says[190], "Remind, because reminding benefits the believers." "You are only to remind." Many of the Prophet's ﷺ teachings were derived from his admonishments and general sermons.

The great Imām Muḥammad Anwar al-Kashmīrī, elaborated on the perspective of 'reminding' in the context of the Prophet's ﷺ ways of teaching. He also distinguished between the functions of the preacher and that of the teaching scholar. Due to its benefits, I would like to quote some of it here:

'Preachers and teachers have two distinct functions. The preacher's objective is to involve emotions of his audience and as such use expressions and gestures that excite and motivate them. He does not pay attention to minutiae of the issue or its prerequisites. He will promise and scare, admonish and entice and order and forbid. He does not care about details.

Teachers and scholars, on the other hand, would like to review the issue and teach us what they know about. Applying this issue is not of an immediate concern. They use a language that is precise and unambiguous – a language that will convey the meaning as precisely as possible. They mention all pertaining facts and if they are to preach they will use these facts as tools of their preaching.

Religious leaders play the role of the preacher more than the teacher. Allah said, "You are only to remind. You are not to control them." However, they use a mixture of both as they want to shake off our complacency and instigate us to act. The natural way to this is for the leader to lead by example as is the case with the Prophet ﷺ whose guidance was mostly taken from his deeds. Whatever he ordered people to do; he will do first and people will learn from his actions and thus did not need formal teaching and training. If his way was only theoretical, Islam would not have been propagated.

When he ordered the believers to do something, he would use instinctive language and simple terms without inundating them with details. He simply asked them to do their best to follow these orders. In turn, the companions did their utmost to follow these orders without splitting hairs or being fussy about details.

❖ ḤADĪTH **121:** Tirmidhī, Ibn Mājah and Abū Dāwūd (the text is his) reported[191] on the authority of ʿAbdur Raḥmān ibn ʿAmr as-Sulamī and Ḥujr ibn Ḥujr who said, 'We went to al-ʿIrbāḍ ibn Sāria. We greeted him and said, 'We have come as visitors and learners and to see how is your health. Al-ʿIrbāḍ said, 'One day, the Messenger of Allah ﷺ led us in prayers and then he turned back to us and gave us a very eloquent sermon that brought tears to our eyes and trembling to our hearts. A person said, 'O Messenger of Allah! It looks like a sermon of farewell - what do you advise us to do?' He replied, "I advise you to fear Allah and to listen and obey your leader even if he was an Abyssinian slave. He who will live after me will see many disagreements. You should therefore adhere to my way *Sunnah* and the way *Sunnah* of the Rightly Guided Caliphs – hold to it even with your teeth. Be wary I warn you not to introduce alien elements into your religion. Every such introduction is an innovation to the religion. Every such innovation is a falsehood."'

❖ ḤADĪTH **122:** Nasā'ī, Ibn Mājah and Muslim (the text is his) reported[192] on the authority of Jābir ibn ʿAbdullah al-Anṣārī (may Allah be pleased with both of them), who said, 'When the Messenger of Allah ﷺ delivered a sermon, his eyes would become red, his voice would be raised and his excitement would show, as though he was warning about an impending army, saying, "It will attack in the morning. If not; in the evening."

And he would say, "I and the Hour were sent like these two", he would then join his index and middle finger.

And he would say, "As for what follows. The best speech is the Book of Allah. The best guidance is the guidance of Muḥammad. The worst of matters is introducing alien elements to the religion and every such innovation is a falsehood."

He would then say, "I will take care of every believer more than he would. Whoever leaves wealth, it is for his family. Whoever leaves a debt or incurred a loss, come to me and I'll pay it."'

Using persuasion & forewarning

The most recurring method in the teachings of the Prophet ﷺ was persuasion toward the good he is advocating and forewarning against the evil he is discouraging. The Prophet ﷺ encouraged the good by telling its rewards and pointing out its benefits. He discouraged evil by mentioning its punishment and pointing out its harms.

In his sermons and speeches the Prophet ﷺ used to combine both persuasion and warning. He would not confine himself to warning against evil alone, as this would alienate the people. Nor would he confine himself to persuasion, for this would lead to laziness and procrastination.

The scholars of ḥadīth have compiled entire books from the noble Traditions *Sunnah* of the Prophet ﷺ devoted solely to these two themes. The most extensive collection, most beneficial, well-known and readily available in print is The Persuasion and Discouragement of the Noble ḥadīth *at-Targhīb wa-t-Tarhīb min al-*ḥ*adīth ash-Sharīf,* of Imām ʿAbdul ʿAẓīm al-Mundhirī.

In preceding reviews of other methods, I have cited many ḥadīths on these two themes to the extent that it becomes redundant to cite them again.

Using stories and ancient history

Frequently, the Prophet ﷺ taught his companions by narrating to them stories and events of previous nations. This would have the best results in guiding his audience and would gain their interest and attention. They enjoyed listening to it and their hearts readily absorbed it since it did not contain orders or prohibitions. It was stories about other nations and people from which one indirectly derives lessons, admonitions, ideals and examples. This follows Allah's method in teaching His Prophet ﷺ. Allah said[193], "All that We relate to you of the accounts of the messengers whereby we console your heart."

Among these stories is the ḥadīth of the Prophet ﷺ urging

people to love each other solely for the sake of Allah and sincere brotherhood for the sake of general good and Islam.

❖ ḤADĪTH **123:** Muslim reported[194] on the authority of Abū Hurayra ‎ that 'the Prophet ‎ said, "A man went to visit a brother in another village. Allah sent an angel [in the form of a human] in his way and when the man reached him, the angel asked, 'Where are you going to?' He replied, 'I am going to visit a brother of mine in this village.' The angel said, 'Is that because you hope to gain something from him?' The man replied, 'No. I just love him for the sake of Allah, Mighty and Majestic is He.' The angel said, 'I'm the envoy of Allah to tell you that Allah loved you because you loved your brother for the sake of Allah."'

Another example of the Prophet using stories and past events is his ḥadīth urging kindness and mercy to animals and warning them against harming and abusing them:

❖ ḤADĪTH **124:** Bukhārī and Muslim (the text is his) reported[195] on the authority of Abū Hurayra that 'the Messenger of Allah said, "While a man was travelling on the road, he felt very thirsty. He found a well and so he went down it, drank and climbed back up. He saw a dog panting and licking, out of thirst, the moist earth. The man said to himself, 'This dog is as thirsty as I was!' He went down the well and filled his shoes with water, held it with his mouth till he climbed out and then gave the water to the dog. Allah was grateful for him and forgave his sins." The companions asked, 'O Messenger of Allah! Are we rewarded for kindness to animals?' The Prophet replied, "For every living being there is a reward."'

❖ ḤADĪTH **125:** Bukhārī and Muslim reported[196] on the authority of Abū Hurayra that 'the Messenger of Allah said, "Whilst a dog was circling a well almost dying out of thirst, an immoral woman from the Israelites saw it and took off her shoe, tied it to her scarf, drew water for the dog and gave it to drink. For this she was forgiven her sins."'

❖ ḤADĪTH 126: Muslim and Bukhārī (the text is his) reported[197] on the authority of ʿAbdullah ibn ʿUmar (may Allah be pleasd with both of them) that 'the Messenger of Allah ﷺ said, "A woman was punished for strapping a cat till it died. She entered hell because of the cat. She neither fed it nor did she let it eat rodents or insects of the earth."'

❖ ḤADĪTH 127: Bukhārī and Muslim (the text is his) reported[198] on the authority of Abū Hurayra ﷺ that the Prophet ﷺ said, "Only three infants spoke in the cradle:

Jesus the son of Mary,

The alleged child of Jurayj. Jurayj was a monk devoted to worship in his hermitage. One time his mother came while he was praying and called him, 'O Jurayj!' He said, 'My Lord! My mother or my prayer?' He continued praying and his mother left.

The next day she came while he was praying and called out, 'O Jurayj!' He said, 'O My Lord! My mother or my prayer?' He continued praying and his mother left. The third day she came while he was praying and called out 'O Jurayj!' He said, 'My Lord! My mother or my prayer?' He continued praying. She said, 'O My Lord! Let him not die before he looks at the faces of prostitutes!'

One day some in the Israelites talked about Jurayj and his devotion. A very attractive prostitute proposed to the Israelites, 'If you wish, I can tempt Jurayj.' She set out to lure him, but he did not pay any attention to her. Hence, she approached a shepherd who used to stay close to the hermitage and offered him to sleep with her and she became pregnant. When she gave birth, she said, 'This is Jurayj's child.' The Israelites went to Jurayj in his hermitage, got him down, destroyed the cell and started beating him. He asked, 'What is wrong with you all?' They said, 'You have fornicated with this prostitute and she delivered a baby from you!' Jurayj said, 'Where is the baby?' And they brought the baby to him. He asked, 'let me just pray.' Jurayj prayed and went to the baby and pointed to his belly with his hand asking, 'O baby! Who is your father?' The baby said, 'My father is the shepherd.' The Israelites started kissing Jurayj and seeking his blessings. They asked him, 'We'll rebuild your hermitage out of gold?' He said, 'Just rebuild it of mud as it was.' And so they did.

Whilst an infant, from the Israelites, who was suckling from his mother, a finely dressed knight passed by. His mother said, 'O Allah, make my child like him.' The infant left her breast, looked at the knight and said, 'O Allah, don't make me like him.' He then returned to her breast and resumed suckling.

Abū Hurayra said, 'As if I am now seeing the Messenger of Allah ﷺ sucking his forefinger in his mouth.'

He said, 'then a group came pulling and beating a slave girl and shouting at her, 'Thief! Fornicator!' and all she was saying is, 'Allah is Sufficient for me and He is the Best Protector.' The mother said, 'O Allah, don't make my child like her.' The infant left her breast, looked at the slave and then said, 'O Allah, make me like her.'

The mother asked, 'How strange! A finely dressed knight passed by and you said, 'O Allah, don't make me like him.' They pulled and beat a slave-girl and shouted at her, 'Thief! Fornicator!' I said, 'O Allah, don't make my son like her,' and you said, 'O Allah, make me like her!'

The infant said, 'The knight was a tyrant, so I said, 'O Allah, don't make me like him.' They were beating the slave girl and shouting 'fornicator,' and she didn't fornicate. They were shouting 'thief,' but she didn't steal. Thus, I said 'O Allah, make me like her."'

We need no further elaboration after these true stories and real events. Its guidance prompts us, through persuasion and warning, to do good and abhor evil. However, some scholarly comments are due.

Ibn Ḥajar, in his Commentary on Bukhārī, said the ḥadīth indicated that voluntary prayers should be interrupted at the call of the mother. Such prayers are optional whilst answering the mother is not. When the third infant was wishing to be like that slave-girl, he was wishing to be like her; free of all sins and not to face allegation while he is innocent.

Subtle preparation prior to teaching sensitive issues

At times the Prophet ﷺ would commence with subtle preparation if he was to teach his companions a sensitive matter that may cause embarrassment.

❖ ḤADĪTH **128:** Muslim, Abū Dāwūd, an-Nasā'ī and Ibn Mājah (the text is his) reported[199] on the authority of Abū Hurayra ﷺ who said, 'The Messenger of Allah ﷺ said, "I am to you like a father is to his child. I am teaching you. When you go out to relieve yourselves, then you should neither face the *qiblah* or turn your backs to it.' He ordered us to use three stones and prohibited the use of dung and bones and he also prohibited a person to cleanse himself with his right hand."'

The Prophet ﷺ ordered three stones to be used for cleansing excrement because that is usually attained by this number. Cleansing with water, when available, is preferable. The use of dung is prohibited because it is an impurity in itself. The ḥadīth provides us with a few points to ponder and to follow:

The humbleness of the Prophet ﷺ.

How considerate the Prophet ﷺ was with those learning at his hand.

How tactful and subtle the Prophet ﷺ was when teaching embarrassing or sensitive topics.

The Prophet ﷺ taught Muslims to follow certain etiquettes and order in all their matters and affairs, including personal hygiene.

When the Prophet ﷺ said he was, to the believers, like a father is to his children, he meant in kindness and affection and in teaching indispensable information. Just as a father teaches manners to his child.

The Prophet ﷺ said, I am teaching you what you have to do. The Prophet ﷺ gave this introduction to inform them that it is his duty to teach them religious issues as it is the duty of a father to teach his child all what he needs to learn – even if it was something embarrassing. The Prophet ﷺ then proceeded to teach them personal hygiene which is not a usual topic to bring up especially in the presence of respected and senior people.

The Prophet ﷺ with this kind introduction broke barriers that may make some of his companions reluctant to ask private, sensitive, or embarrassing questions.

That the Prophet ﷺ is like a father from another perspective. As parents are the source of many guidance and blessings, the Prophet ﷺ is the source of our salvation and guidance for the eternal life.

Imām Al-Ghazālī in *Iḥyā'* said, 'For this reason the rights of the teacher have become greater than the rights of the parents. The parents are the cause of the children's present existence in this mortal life, while the teacher is the basis of their eternal life. If it is not for the teacher, parents' ways may lead to eternal destruction. Only the teacher brings the eternal life in the next world. By teacher, I mean the teacher of the sciences of the religion or the sciences of this world, whose goal is the delight in the hereafter and not the glitter of this world. Teaching with the sole view of achieving success in this world is a loss and devastation from which we seek refuge with Allah.'

IMPLICITLY REFERRING TO SENSITIVE TOPICS

On certain occasions, the Prophet ﷺ would implicitly refer to issues that may bring embarrassment if mentioned explicitly.

❖ ḤADĪTH 129: Bukhārī and Muslim reported[200] on the authority of ʿĀ'isha ﷺ that, Asmā' bint Shakal asked the Prophet ﷺ about taking a bath at the end of her period. The Prophet said, "One of you should take water and pounded leaves of the Nabk tree and cleanse herself thoroughly. She should then pour water onto her head and rub it vigorously so that water reaches the roots of her hair. She should then pour water over her entire body. She should then take a piece of cotton fragranced with musk and cleanse herself with it."

Asmā' asked, 'How should she cleanse herself with it?' The Prophet replied, "Glory be to Allah! Cleanse yourself with it!" ʿĀ'isha said almost in whispering that, 'Follow the trace of blood.'

She asked him about taking a bath after a major impurity. The Prophet said, "She should take water and bathe well" or he said, "bathe thoroughly. Then she should pour water onto her head and rub it until water reaches the roots of her hair, She should then pour water over her entire body."

ʿĀ'isha said, 'The best are the women of the Anṣār! Shyness did not prevent them from learning their religion.'

When Asmā' asked how she should cleanse herself with fragrance cotton, the Prophet ﷺ did not respond by elaborating as it is too intimate and embarrassing. He just said "Glory be to Allah," to express his wonder about what she was asking and that should be known to women like her.

In this ḥadīth, the Prophet ﷺ pointed out to her the additional preference when taking a bath after menstruation; to add Nabk leaves into the water. And then to perfume the place of the blood.

In addition, the ḥadīth brings other points.

The teacher may praise Allah to show his surprise, something commonly used among Muslims. The implicit meaning is praising Allah who created us differently so that you not know such an obvious matter - which does not need much thought to recognise it.

A woman may ask a male scholar about matters that might be embarrassing to her.

It is preferable to resort to hints and symbolic language when teaching aspects that are related to private parts, etc...

It is preferable to resort to hints and symbolic language when answering questions that has answers that may embarrass the listeners or too inappropriate for the situation.

Repeating an answer to make it fully understood. Here, the Prophet ﷺ repeated the answer even though she did not understand it the first time because his gesture of turning his face away when he said to her, "cleanses yourself with it." As it is not appropriate to be explicit, ʿĀ'isha understood what the Prophet ﷺ meant and explained it to the lady.

One may explain the words of a scholar in his presence to someone who did not understand it, but only if he knew that the scholar will be pleased with that.

One may learn from a less learned person, ʿĀ'isha in this case, in the presence of a more learned person, namely the Prophet ﷺ.

The validity of a student reading or reviewing a topic to the teacher if the latter let it pass even if he did not expressly say 'yes' after the reading or the review.

A student may pass on knowledge even if he did not understand everything that he has heard. Teachers should be kind and considerate with students who did not understand them. A person should conceal his flaws, even natural ones. Here, the Prophet ﷺ asked the woman to cleanse herself to remove the odour.

When answering an embarrassing question, the teacher should not address the enquirer directly. Here, the Prophet ﷺ said to her, "One of you should take..." instead of "you should..." This shows additional tact and consideration in this situation.

The noble character of the Prophet ﷺ; the greatest teacher. How kind, gentle and considerate he was. May Allah increase him in honour and status.

Teaching and educating women

The Prophet ﷺ paid particular attention to teaching women all what they needed to learn. He therefore used to have exclusive lectures and sermons for them.

❖ ḤADĪTH **130:** Bukhārī and Muslim (the text is his) reported[201] on the authority of Ibn ʿAbbās (may Allah be pleased with both of them) who said, 'I bear witness that the Messenger of Allah ﷺ prayed the *Eid* prayer before the sermon. When he delivered the sermon and felt that his voice did not reach the women, he went to them, reminded them, admonished them and asked them to give in charity while Bilāl spread his cloth and the women began throwing their rings, earrings and other items.'

The ḥadīth recommends teaching and lecturing women and to remind them of the hereafter, the injunctions of Islam and to urge them to give in charity. This, however, should be done in a way that does not cause temptations on both sides.

The ḥadīth recommends the separation of women and men at prayers and large gatherings.

❖ ḤADĪTH **131:** Bukhārī and Muslim reported[202] on the authority of Abū Sa'īd al-Khudrī ﷺ who said, 'Some women said to the Prophet ﷺ, 'Men are getting much of your time, so set aside a day for us.' So he promised them a day where he would meet them and give them religious lessons and commandments.

Once during such a lesson he said, "A woman whose three children die will be shielded by them from the Hellfire." On that a woman asked, 'If only two die? Two, Two' The Messenger of Allah ﷺ replied, 'Even two. Two, two."'

USING ANGER AND REPRIMAND IF APPROPRIATE

The Prophet ﷺ would occasionally get very angry if a student, in his questions and research, went beyond limits to what could not be fathomed or understood.

❖ ḤADĪTH **132:** Ibn Mājah reported[203] on the authority of ᶜAbdullah ibn ᶜAmr ibn al-ᶜĀṣ (may Allah be pleased with both of them) who said, 'The Messenger of Allah ﷺ came to his companions while they were arguing about pre-destiny. His face became so red with anger and he said, "Is this what you have been ordered? Or is this what you have been created for? Contradicting the Qur'ān with the Qur'ān! This is what doomed ancient nations before." ᶜAbdullah ibn ᶜAmr said, 'I never congratulated myself for missing a meeting with the Messenger of Allah ﷺ except on missing that one."

The Prophet ﷺ became angry with his companions because they were arguing about fate and pre-destiny which is one of the mysteries that only Allah knows fully. Attempting to understand such issues is prohibited since it may lead to more puzzlement and misunderstanding. As the creatures of Allah, we should accept His orders without trying to reach what we cannot reach with our human senses.

In a narration by Imām Aḥmad, the Prophet ﷺ directed them to be practical in their faith and steer away from such futile arguments, "Look at what I commanded you to do and do it. What I forbid you to do then cease doing it."

❖ ḤADĪTH 133: Tirmidhī reported on the authority of Abū Hurayra ﷺ who said, 'The Messenger of Allah ﷺ came out to us while we were arguing about fate and pre-destiny. His face became red with anger. He then said, "Is this what you have been ordered to do? Is this what I have been sent to you with? Those who were before you were doomed when they argued about this matter. I emphasise upon you, I emphasise upon you that you do not argue about this."'

Using writing for teaching and dissemination

The Prophet ﷺ used writing as a method of teaching despite being among people who could not read or write. The Prophet ﷺ had more than 15 scribes who used to write down the Qur'ān as it was being revealed to him. He had other scribes exclusively assigned to write his letters to different states and rulers, explaining Islam to them and inviting them to join it. Beside those, he had yet other scribes assigned to other tasks. All this could be learned in further details from the book of my Shaikh, the Ḥāfiẓ of Maghrib, Shaikh ʿAbdul Hayy al-Kattānī 'The Management of the Prophet' *at-Tarātīb al-Idāriyya.*

The four Rightly Guided Caliphs, Abū Bakr, ʿUmar, ʿUthmān and ʿAlī were among the scribes to whom the Prophet ﷺ dictated the Qur'ān as it was revealed to him. In addition, there was Zayd ibn Thābit, Ubayy ibn Kaʿb, Zubayr ibn al-ʿAwwām, Khālid ibn Saʿīd ibn al-ʿĀṣ, his brother Abān ibn Saʿīd ibn al-ʿĀṣ, Ḥanẓala ibn ar-Rabī', Muʿāwiya ibn Abī Sufyān and others. When a part of the Qur'ān was revealed, the Prophet ﷺ would summon one of them and write what the Prophet ﷺ dictated verbatim.

It is also established that the Prophet ﷺ allowed some of his companions to write down his ḥadīth. In fact, he even ordered some of them to write it down.

❖ ḤADĪTH **134:** Abū Dāwūd reported[204] on the authority of ᶜAbdullah ibn ᶜAmr ibn al-ᶜĀṣ (may Allah be pleased with both of them) who said, 'I used to write down everything I used to hear from the Messenger of Allah ﷺ if I wanted to memorise. But the Quraysh forbade me from doing this and said, 'Are you going to write down everything that you hear? And the Messenger of Allah ﷺ is a human - he speaks in anger and in happiness!' So I stopped writing. I then mentioned this to the Messenger of Allah ﷺ and he pointed with his finger to his mouth and said, "Write for by He who has my soul in His hand; nothing but the truth emanates from it."'

❖ ḤADĪTH **135:** Muslim and Bukhārī (the text is his) reported[205] on the authority of Abū Hurayra ﷺ who said that, 'when Allah gave His messenger ﷺ victory over Makkah, He gave a speech to the people. He praised Allah and glorified Him, he then said, "Allah held back the elephant from Makkah and allowed it for His messenger and the believers but no one is allowed to do that after me. Its animals should not be chased, its thorny trees should not be cut and its lost articles should not be picked up except by he who will announce it and seek its owner. He whose relative has been killed has one of two options: accepting financial compensation or seeking punishment."

Al-ᶜAbbās said, 'Except Sweet Rush *Idhkhir* for we use it in our graves and houses.' The Messenger of Allah ﷺ said, "Except the Sweet Rush."

Abū Shāh, a man from Yemen, stood up and said, 'Write for me, O Messenger of Allah!' And the Messenger of Allah ﷺ said, "Write for Abū Shāh."

I said to al-Awzā'ī, 'what does he mean by, 'Write for me O Messenger of Allah?'' He said, 'this is the sermon I heard from the Messenger of Allah ﷺ.'

❖ ḤADĪTH **136:** Bukhārī reported[206] on the authority of Abū Juḥaifa who said, 'I asked 'Alī, 'Do you have something written?' He replied, 'No, except the Book of Allah, an insight bestowed on a Muslim, or what is written on this page.' He said, 'I asked, 'What is written on this page?' He replied, 'Compensation, the freeing of a prisoner and that a Muslim will not be killed on account of an unbeliever.''

The reason for the question of Abū Juḥaifa if ʿAlī had anything written down from the Prophet ﷺ is that some of the Shīʿa claimed that the family of the Prophet ﷺ especially ʿAlī had some divine revelation which the Prophet ﷺ gave exclusively to them while he did reveal it to others.

Beside these quoted samples, the Prophet ﷺ sent, under his name, many letters to different lands and rulers. Some of them were an invitation to Islam and belief in Allah. Others were lists of the rules and injunctions of Islam for those who newly embraced Islam. The Prophet's ﷺ biographies and books of ḥadīth and history have saved these splendid letters and messages.

The Prophet ﷺ ordered his companions to learn foreign languages

❖ ḤADĪTH **137:** Bukhārī and Tirmidhī (the text is his) reported[207] that Zaid ibn Thābit ﷺ said, 'The Messenger of Allah ﷺ ordered me to learn for him some vocabulary from the language of the Jews. He said to me, "By Allah, I do not trust Jews with my writing." He said, 'I learnt it within half a month. After I learnt it, if he was to write to the Jews, I would write the letter. And if they wrote to him, I would read their letter to him.'

The utilisation of foreign languages for teaching and propagation of Islam when needed has its roots in the Sunnah of the Prophet ﷺ and as such falls within the teaching methods of the Prophet ﷺ.

Today, learning languages is a key to modern sciences that have become indispensable for progress and prosperity. It is also the key to international cooperation and protection of rights and properties. Shaikh Ṣafiyy ad-Dīn al-Ḥillī who knew several languages said in a poem:

> The more languages you master, the more useful you are
> The languages are your helpers in difficulties
> Hasten, then, to learn new languages.
> Each language learned makes and creates a new personality for you.

Teaching through personality

The Prophet ﷺ was a teacher whom Allah selected to teach humanity the religion of Allah and His final and eternal laws. For this most valuable and important task, to communicate and teach this religion, Allah selected the finest of Prophets and Messengers - Muḥammad ﷺ.

This teacher Allah has chosen to convey His *Sharīʿa* to humanity, taught by his appearance and inner self, his talk and conduct and all his life under different circumstances. The perfection of his noble personality is, in itself, a teaching method all other teachers should emulate and follow.

The most important requirements of a teacher is to possess the highest qualities of intellect, virtues, knowledge, wisdom, appearance, elegance, tact, movements and gestures, good speech, nice smell, clean clothes, appealing appearance, eloquence and all aspects of conduction himself.

All these qualities were present, in a perfect form and best grace in the personality of the Messenger - the teacher. Through his honoured and exemplary personality, he was a teacher to every teacher and educator. He is a complete embodiment of teaching methods that aim to bring out Muslims who fulfil the description of the Qur'ān, "You were the best nation brought forth from humanity." This all-embracing perfection of the Prophet ﷺ in all methods of teaching is the ultimate essence of teaching and instruction. His noble personality merited the highest and the most magnificent and unique praise - fully emphasised by Allah, "Indeed, You enjoy the best of manners."[208]

It is therefore only normal to count his many noble qualities among his teaching methods. For there was no other teacher who had such an impact on humanity whereby people of different races and cultures embraced his religion and laws and took him as an exemplary model in all aspects of their lives.

There are few words that I would like to make in the conclusion of the teaching methods of the Prophet ﷺ, forty methods so far, to crown the previous pages. These are just examples of what teaching methods the Prophet ﷺ used and provided for us to follow. These are by no means comprehensive of every teaching method he used, but it will open our eyes to his greatness in all aspects of his life and will provide us with nice examples to follow.

I have no doubt that researchers and students of the ḥadīth and noble biography of the Prophet ﷺ will be able to shed light on other methods which I have not covered here, for this book is based on what I came across in the course of my reading and studies.

I pray to Allah to guide me to success and sincerity and to grant me the intercession of the leader of people, Muḥammad ﷺ. I ask Allah to be pleased with this work and to accept it and to give me the honour to follow the Sunnah of the Prophet ﷺ. I ask Him to be pleased with the Prophet's ﷺ noble companions and those who follow them in good till the Day of Resurrection. All praise is due to Allah, the Sustainer of the worlds.

NOTES

1. The Qur'ān, Sūra al-Jumuʿah, 62:2.
2. The Qur'ān, Sūra an-Nisā', 4:79.
3. The Qur'ān, Sūra Sabā', 34:28.
4. Muḥammad ibn Yazid Ibn Mājah al-Qazwini, *Sunan Ibn Mājah*, 1:83. ʿAbdullah ibn Abdul Rahman Al-Darami *Sunan al-Darami,* p. 54. Hafiz al-Khateeb al-Baghdadi reported this ḥadīth on the authority of many narrators in his book *al-Faqīh wa al-Mutafaqih (The Scholar and the Student).* You may refer to it for further research.My Shaykh, te Ḥāfiẓ of Maghrib, Shaykh ʿAbdul Ḥayy al-Kattānī, in his book "The Management of the Prophet" *at-Tarātīb al-Idāriyyah* quoting Al-Ḥāfiẓ as-Sakhawī said that "this ḥadīth is a weak odd one due to the weakness of one of its narrators, Ziyād ibn Anʿam al-Afirqī, who didn't enjoy good memory but the text has similarity with other." I would say that among these texts is the next ḥadīth reported by Imam Muslim.
5. Imam Nawawī, may Allah bless his soul, in his introduction of *Ṣaḥīḥ* Muslim wrote a special chapter on "Recommendation for a scholar of ḥadīth when writing the name of Allah to add "Mighty and Majestic is He *ʿAzza wa Jall*", "Exalted is He *Taʿālā*", "Glorified and Exalted is He *Subḥānahu wa Taʿālā*", "Blessed and Exalted is He *Tabāraka wa Taʿālā*", "Majestic is His remembrance *Jalla Dhikruhu*", "Blessed is His name *Tabāraka-smuhu*" , or "Majestic is His greatness *Jallat ʿAzmatuhu*" or similar words of respect. Likewise, when the Prophet ﷺ is mentioned one should add "Peace and blessings of Allah be upon him *Ṣalla Allahu ʿalayhi wa sallam*".

One should not use abbreviation or part of it. If the name of a companion is mentioned it should be followed by "May Allah be pleased with him, *Raḍiya Allāh ʿAnhu*" even if it was not in the original text since is not a narration but a prayer. One should tirelessly apply this. If he did not, then he missed great blessings and rewards."

6. Thomas Carlyle, *On Heroes, Hero-Worship and Heroic in History*, 1840
7. Muslim ibn al-Ḥajjāj al-Nīsabūrī, *Ṣaḥīḥ Muslim,* 10:81.
8. Muḥammad ibn Muḥammad al-Ghazālī, *Iḥyā' ʿUlūm al-Dīn,* 1:57.
9. Muslim 5:20 in the Book of Prayer, under "The Chapter of the prohibition of speech in the Prayer..."
10. Yaḥyā Ibn Sharaf al-Nawawī, *Commentary of Ṣaḥīḥ Muslim,* 5:30.
11. Aḥmad ibn Idrīs al-Qarāfī, *al-Furūq*, 4:170.
12. ʿAbdul Aẓīm ibn ʿAbdul Qawī al-Mundhirī, *at-Targhīb wa at-Tarhīb, 1:86*. He discussed, in his book *Kanz al-Umal*, the authenticity of this ḥadīth and concluded that, despite having a questionable narrator, it has a valid chain of transmission based on the opinion of Hafiz Ibn al-Sakan.
13. The Qur'ān, Sura al-Maeda 5:78-79
14. The Prophet ﷺ said, "Gabriel continued recommending to me the rights of the neighbour till I thought he would give him some inheritance."
15. Musṭafā az-Zarqā, *al-Madkhal al-Fiqhī al-ʿĀm*, 7th edition, 2:641.
16. Ibn Mājah 1:41. This ḥadīth is considered weak by some scholars. However, it has been reported by so many people that it is considered to be a fair ḥadīth. Imam Suyuṭi and others accepted it.
17. The Qur'ān, Sūra al-ʿAlaq, 96:1-5.
18. The Qur'ān, Sūra an-Nisā', 4:113.
19. Muslim ibn al-Ḥajjāj al-Nīsabūrī, *Ṣaḥīḥ Muslim,* 17:41.
20. The Qur'ān, Sura at-Tawbah, 9:128.
21. Muḥammad Ibn Ismail al-Bukhārī, *Ṣaḥīḥ al-Bukhārī*, 2:93. Muslim, *Ṣaḥīḥ Muslim,* 5:174
22. Muḥammad ibn 'Isā ibn Mūsā at-Tirmidhī, *ash-Shamāi'l,* 140.

23. Ibid.

24. Ibid, 141.

25. This ḥadīth nullifies all deeds that do not conform to the rules of Allah and His Messenger ﷺ. Allah only accepts deeds that are in accordance with these rules.

26. Muḥammad ibn 'Isā ibn Mūsā at-Tirmidhī, *ash-Shamāi'l*, 221-224.

27. Muslim 1:169, 171. Aḥmad ibn Shuʿayb al-Nasā'ī 4:121.

28. al-Tirmidhī, *al-Shamai'l* 212

29. Bukhārī, *al-Adab al-Mufrad*, p. 511. Muslim 6:165. Nasā'ī 8:220

30. Al-Nawawī, *Commentary on Ṣaḥīḥ Muslim*, 6:165

31. Bukhārī 1:148, Nasā'ī 4:122, Ibn Mājah 1:169, Darami 1:130.

32. Muslim 1:172. Bukhārī 3:231. Nasā'ī 1:234.

33. Muslim 15:82. Abū Dāwūd Sulaymān ibn al-Ashʿath, *Sunan Abī Dāwūd*, 4:257. at-Tirmidhī, *Sunan* at-Tirmidhī, 205.

34. An-Nawawī 15:82.

35. This is cited by 'Allāmah al-Qasṭallānī in al-Mawāhib al-Ladaniyyah 4:319 – 320 with the Commentary of az-Zarqānī.

36. This wording is cited by al-Māwardī and by al-Ḥāfiẓ Ibn Ḥajar in *Fatḥ al-Bārī* 8:15 and others. The verse referred to is from Sūrah Yūsuf 12:92.

37. Narrated by Abū Yaʿlā in his Musnad on the authority of ʿUmar ibn al-Khaṭṭāb ﷺ and the chain of narration is good.

38. Sūrah āl ʿImrān 3:110.

39. Reported by ad-Daylamī in al-Firdaous and ibn ʿAsākir in his history on the authority of Anas ibn Mālik ﷺ but with a variance of wordings.

40. I could not find such a ḥadīth with this wording. However, ad-Daylamī in al-Firdaous 2:351 cited, without commenting on its grading, a ḥadīth carrying the same meaning, "Earthly life is a bridge to the Hereafter; cross it but do not dwell it." Also al-Ḥākim in his *Mustadrak* 4:312 cited a ḥadīth, "Life on Earth is good for the one who used it to prepare for pleasing Allah in the Hereafter." Al-Ḥākim graded this ḥadīth as authentic but among its narrators is an unknown person: ʿAbdul Jabbār ibn Wahb.

41. See al-Māwardī who also gathered together different aḥādīth from this type of context.

42. The Qur'ān, 33:21.

43. Al-Ḥajawī, Muḥammad (1291-1376/1874-1956): Noble Review of the Islamic Jurisprudence *al-Fikr as-Sāmī fi Tārīkh al-Fiqh al-Islāmī* 1:154.

44. The Qur'ān, 17:1.

45. The Qur'ān, 25:1.

46. The Qur'ān, 2:23.

47. The Qur'ān, 49:13.

48. Imam ash-Shāṭibī, *al-ᶜItiṣām,* 2:239-240.

49. Muslim 18:136. Abū Dāwūd 1:131.

50. Ibn Ḥajar al-ᶜAsqlanī: Hadi al-Sari 2:196.

51. Tirmidhī 1:102, Nasā'ī 1:258, Ibn Mājah 1:219, Muslim 5:114

52. Muslim 5:114, Tirmidhī 1:102, Nasā'ī 1:258, Ibn Mājah 1:218.

53. Bukhārī 11:213.

54. Muslim 5:35. Bukhārī 1:409 & 2:331. Al-Ḥāfiẓ Ibn Ḥajar, *Fatḥ al-Bārī*, vol. I, p. 228 and vol. II, p. 214.

55. Nawawī. Commentary on *Ṣaḥīḥ* Muslim 5:75.

56. Ibn Ḥajar, *Fatḥ al-Bārī*, 2:331.

57. Abū Dāwūd 1:86, Ibn Mājah 2:1061

58. Ibn Mājah 1:23

59. Bukhārī 3:357, Muslim 1:196.

60. Bukhārī 1:160.

61. Ibn Ḥajar: *Fatḥ al-Bārī* 1:162.

62. Ibn ᶜAbdul Barr, *Jāmiᶜ Bayān al-ᶜIlm* 1:431.

63. al-Musnad 5:410.

64. 1:35.

65. Bukhārī 1:162 and Muslim 17:163.

66. Bukhārī 1:163. Muslim 12:42.

67. Nawawī 12:4l.

93. Bukhārī 2:9 and Muslim 5:170.

94. 1:206 with authentic narration.

95. Muslim 16:135.

96. Muslim 1:157-160 and Bukhārī 1:114 reported this ḥadīth on the authority of Abū Hurayrah. The most exhaustive reference for the various narration of this ḥadīth is Ḥāfiẓ ibn Manda in the beginning of the first volume of "The Book of Faith, *Kitāb al-Īmān*" and Ḥāfiẓ Ibn Ḥajar in his Commentary on Bukhārī 1:115-125.

97. Nawawī: Commentary on Muslim 1:157-158.

98. Nawawī: Commentary on Bukhārī 245-246.

99. Nawawī: Commentary on Muslim 1:158.

100. Nawawī: Commentary on Muslim 1:160.

101. Nawawī: Commentary on Muslim 1:158.

102. Aḥmad 5:256, Ṭabarānī 8 no.7679 and al-Haythamī in *Majmaʿ az-Zawā'id* said, 'the narrators of this ḥadīth are among the narrators of authentic ḥadīth.' Al- Ḥāfiẓ al-ʿIrāqī said in *Takhrīj aḥādīth al-Ahyā'*, 'Aḥmad reported this ḥadīth with reliable narrators who are among the narrators of the authentic aḥādīth.'

103. Bukhārī 1:345. Muslim 2:67.

104. Bukhārī reported this 11 times under different headings in his *Ṣaḥīḥ* 1:133, 1:136, 1:151, 2:203, 4:337, 8:286, 9:492, 9:495, 10:435, 10:443. Muslim reported it 5 times 17:153-155. The text here is a combination of the narrations of Bukhārī and Muslim.

105. This was cited by ʿAbdul al-Ḥayy al-Kittānī, my Shaykh and master scholar ḥadīth in Morocco, in his book 'the Prophet Administration *at-Tartīb al-Idāriyyah*' 2:232.

106. Bukhārī 5:44.

107. Muslim 7:91.

108. Abū Dāwūd 3:341. Tirmidhī 3:519. Nasā'ī 7:269Ṭ Ibn Mājah 2:761.

109. Abū Dāwūd 4:357. It is reported by Bukhārī 9:65 and Muslim 6:83.

110. Ibn al-Qayyim, *Miftāḥ Dar as-Saʿādah, The Key to the Abode of Happiness*, 1:55.

111. Bukhārī 1:175. Muslim 15:46.

112. As quoted by Ḥāfiẓ Ibn Ḥajar in his Commentary on Bukhārī 1:177. The quoted book remains a manuscript that has not been published.
113. pp. 57-59.
114. 15:48.
115. Bukhārī 5:132 & 5:292 (the quote here combines both narrations). Tirmidhī 3:318.
116. *Fatḥ al-Bārī* 5:295-296.
117. An-Nasā'ī 8:124.
118. Musnad 3:397 & Marwazī 6. The narration here is a combination of both.
119. The Qur'ān, Surat al-Anʿām 6:153.
120. Bukhārī 11:202.
121. 1:293, 316 & 322.
122. Bukhārī 5:72 and 10:376 and Muslim 16:139.
123. Muslim 8:178.
124. Bukhārī 9:389 and 10:365.
125. Bukhārī 6:344-348 and Muslim 16:106-108.
126. Aḥmad 1:458.
127. 2:252 and 253.
128. Al- Ḥāfiẓ al-Haythamī. *Mawārid az-Zam'an* to Zawā'id ibn Hibban, 63.
129. Abū Dāwūd 4:50, Nasā'ī 8:160, and Ibn Mājah 2:1189.
130. Aḥmad 5:330. Its chain of narrators is acceptable.
131. Bukhārī 6:240 and 13:230 and Muslim 2:154.
132. 4:231.
133. 1:286.
134. Bukhārī 1:187 (he reported this ḥadīth under 11 headings). Muslim 15:112.
135. 1:421. This ḥadīth is supported by a second ḥadīth reported also by Abū Dāwūd on the authority of Ibn ʿAbbās. Ibn Mājah also re-

ported a similar ḥadīth 1:189.

136. Muslim 16:111.

137. Muslim 1:165.

138. The Qur'ān 84:7-8.

139. Bukhārī 9:633 and 638 and Muslim 13:122.

140. Mālik 1:22 and Abū Dāwūd 1:21.

141. Muslim 9:99, Abū Dāwūd 2:194 and Nasā'ī 5:120.

142. Bukhārī 7:40, 10:463 and 13:116 and Muslim 16:185.

143. Turmeric (Curcuma longa), a member of the ginger family, is a spice and a fabric dye.

144. Bukhārī 1:197, 6:21 and 159 and Muslim 13:49.

145. Muslim 13:28 and Nasā'ī 6:34.

146. Bukhārī 12:345-379, Muslim 15:28, Abū Dāwūd 4:288, Tirmidhī 3:252 and Ibn Mājah 2:1289.

147. Nawawī, Commentary on Muslim 15:19. For more on this ḥadīth see: Ibn Ḥajar, Commentary on Bukhārī 12:381-383.

148. Aḥmad 2:185. Darqutnī 4:203. Ibn Ḥajar, in his Commentary on Bukhārī, ranked this ḥadīth as a weak ḥadīth.

149. Musnad Aḥmad 4:205 and Darqutnī 4:203.

150. Ibn Mājah 2:785 and Darqutnī 4:229.

151. Muslim 6:93.

152. Al-Baqarah 2:255.

153. Abū Dāwūd 3:303, Tirmidhī 6:68, Daramī 1:55, Ibn Saʿd 2:737 and Wakʿi, Stories of Judges 1:98.

154. Abū Dāwūd 1:141.

155. Al-Nisā' 4:29.

156. Muslim 18:93.

157. Bukhārī 10:360 and Muslim 17:70.

158. Al-Baqarah 2:207.

159. Qāf 50:39.

160. Tirmidhī 3:241.

161. As quoted by Ibn ʿAllān in his Commentary on Adhkār *al-futuḥat ar-rabāniyyah ʿala al-adhkār an-nawawiyyah* 6:297.

162. Nawawī *al-Adhkār* p. 29.

163. Bukhārī 1:826, Muslim 14:128, Tirmidhī 2:128, Ibn Mājah 2:1231 and Abū Dāwūd 4:293.

164. Abū Dāwūd 4:300 and Tirmidhī 6:215.

165. Ibn al-Qayyim. *Ilam al-Muwaqīn* 4:165. *Zād al-Maʿād* 2:313.

166. Respectively: Yūnus 10:53, Sabā' 34:3 and at-Taghābun 64:7.

167. Muslim 2:35.

168. Muslim 2:17.

169. Bukhārī 10:370.

170. Bukhārī 1:188-189.

171. Ibn Ḥajar 1:189.

172. Bukhārī 1:196.

173. Ibn Ḥajar 1:197.

174. Bukhārī 1:188.

175. Bukhārī 1:189.

176. Aḥmad 5:245-246.

177. Ibn Ḥajar 10:412.

178. Muslim 1:229 and Bukhārī 6:44, 10:334, 11:52, 11:290 and 13:300. Ibn Ḥajar elaborated extensively on the fourth narration of Bukhārī.

179. Muslim 4:118 and Bukhārī 11:56.

180. Muslim 5:15.

181. Aḥmad 3:166. It is also reported by ʿAbdur Razzāq in his *Musannaf* 11:287 and by Ibn al-Mubārak in *az-Zuhud* p. 241. The text quoted here is taken mostly from al-Mundhirī's *at-Targīb wa at-Tarhīb* 5:178.

182. For a detailed research on this topic see the excellent book of our teacher Shaykh Muḥammad ʿAbdul Wahhāb Buhayrī in his books 'Ploys in Islamic Laws.'

183. Bukhārī 3:238 and 5:252, Muslim 7:18 and Ibn Mājah 1:478.

184. Muslim 7:20.
185. Bukhārī 10:370. This ḥadīth came previously under number 105.
186. Muslim 16:108.
187. Al-Ḥākim, *al-Mustadrak* 4:306.
188. Bukhārī 9:132 and Muslim 10:51.
189. Nawawī 10:52.
190. In chapter 51, verse 55 and chapter 88, verse 21.
191. Tirmidhī 4:150, Ibn Mājah 1:15 and Abū Dāwūd 4:280-281.
192. Nasā'ī 3:188, Ibn Mājah 1:17 and Muslim 6:153-156.
193. The Qur'ān 11:120.
194. Muslim 16:124.
195. Bukhārī 10:366 and Muslim 14:241.
196. Bukhārī 6:256 and Muslim 14:242.
197. Bukhārī 6:380 and Muslim 14:240.
198. Bukhārī 6:344-348 and Muslim 16:106-108.
199. Muslim 3:153, Abū Dāwūd 1:30, Nasā'ī 1:38 and Ibn Mājah 1:114.
200. Bukhārī 1:353 and 354 and Muslim 4:15.
201. Bukhārī 1:192 and Muslim 6:173.
202. Bukhārī 1:195 and Muslim 16:181.
203. Ibn Mājah 1:33.
204. Abū Dāwūd 3:434.
205. Muslim 9:128 and Bukhārī 1:205 and 5:87.
206. Bukhārī 1:204.
207. Bukhārī 13:185 and Tirmidhī 4:167.
208. The Qur'ān, 68:4.